TABLE OF CC

FOREWORD

There are many different concepts surrounding money and wealth.

Many of them suggest that working on your dreams and doing something you're passionate about is the ideal; as it can be equally lucrative as it is rewarding, in comparison to a typical 9 till 5 job.

Other ideas conclude that starting your own business is a worthwhile endeavour. With added control over your time, and the freedom to make your own decisions, this path has the ability to make you happier through earning money alongside the ease of living on your own terms.

Many of these notions will likely say things such as - stop giving up your time for money or
encourage learning how to generate multiple sources of passive income.

The big one that really hits home for most people is the suggestion that your worth, financially speaking, is underpinned by your perceived value to the marketplace. The "marketplace" being the consumers of the products and services available within the market. Family, friends, and employers all fall under the idea of the consumer. Your value is usually determined by the problem you can solve. The size of the problem, and the demand for it being solved are both crucial variables in establishing your value.

Personally, I buy into the beliefs discussed above. The idea of managing my own time, as well as having no limit on the amount of money I can potentially generate is appealing to me. Furthermore, as someone who enjoys being creative in my problem solving, the freedom of decision making is equally as enticing. However, it is inevitable that many of these ideas come with a certain level of risk whilst being incredibly demanding - particularly in the beginning. So, although these are all excellent ideas in theory, in practice they may not be for everyone. With that being said, I have met many people who are fulfilled in their regular job, equipped with their set hours, salary, and someone to report to. Synonymous with job security, this style of work can provide enough money to allow for the life they aspire to have. Though this kind of work isn't as glamourised as the entrepreneurial lifestyle, it has its own benefits, and still allows you to accumulate wealth over time. With the correct resources, you'll be able to come to an informed decision on how you'd prefer to make money, learning which style of work complements you.

However, the purpose of this book is not to tell you how to make your money. My aim is to help you understand the array of important actions to take with your money once you acquire it - regardless of whether you are a millionaire business owner or if you are person that works a salaried job, and in that case, regardless of your salary. The importance of these actions cannot be understated, they can be the difference between your financial success (however you define that) and your downfall.

It goes without saying that everyone will be at different stages of wealth and work, and consequently will have different starting points. After reading this book, you will be able to realise what stage you are at, and the following steps that you need to start taking to ensure solid financial grounding, on which to build wealth for the future.

I have never understood why they don't teach this in schools and since understanding how to manage my money and implementing these actions, I wish I'd learnt much sooner.

Also, it must be appreciated that 'Financial Wellness' is an integral part of our overall health and mental well-being. For most people, uncertainty around money is a major contribution to everyday stress and anxiety.

"Money is inextricably linked to our mental, emotional and physical health. In fact, the Office of National Statistics Opinions and Lifestyle survey has outlined that emotional wellbeing, unemployment and financial stability are the top three worries that affect people across the UK."

\-   *Source: www.maddyness.co.uk*

INTRODUCTION

My Mission

I believe there are lessons in this book that will be valuable to anyone that reads it.

However, my personal mission is to make sure that every person has the tools to financially safeguard their future. Particularly those who are underprivileged or disadvantaged in some way.

I want to make sure that everybody regardless of their start in life or how much money they have, has access to the information in a simple and easy way to understand, so that they have a good fighting chance for financial success too.

Dedicated to, and in loving memory of...

Kobe Lee Hannam

15/08/2001 - 29/12/2021

A special message for my amazing little brother who is sadly no longer with us anymore.

The reason I dedicate this work to you is because you were one of the biggest reasons for my drive and that drive helped me to learn so many things about myself that would not have been possible without it. It's a significant part of the reason I am the person I am today and why I am even able to write this book.

It's hard to think that the suffering you endured in your life is a huge part of the reason that I have the ability to truly appreciate mine.

Despite your disabilities and your needs - in my eyes you gave far more than you took - I owe you everything and I hope I can make you proud!

I love you bro & I miss you every day.

Fly free... And wherever you are...

Keep On Beating Expectations #KOBE

What is Flow State Money about and what to expect?

Flow State Money has multiple messages and lessons, but it's really about living your life with peace-of-mind and confidence. When you know exactly what you are doing and when you need to do it, you get a feeling of certainty, and this alone can help overcome any feelings of anxiety and worry. Building your financial grounding is at the core of this, regardless of how much money you earn. Financial success means something different to everyone. Whatever it means to you, understanding how to structure your financial grounding is the key to financial success and supporting the life you want and love to live. Allowing you to enjoy life now as well as secure your financial future.

We have all heard the saying that money does not make you happy and I believe this to be true in some respects. However, money is a tool that is used to bring us so many of the experiences in life that contribute to our happiness. An example of this could your dream home, where you have enough space to entertain special occasions with friends and family and create amazing memories. Or, perhaps it's helping, or doing something special for a loved one. Simple things such as going to the gym or going on holiday (activities that encourage a healthy physical and mental wellbeing) all cost money. Our financial capabilities are at the core of so many things in our lives that bring us joy, so it is imperative that we understand how to manage our personal finances effectively. If this area of our lives is not in control, it can have a knock-on effect on every other area of our lives. This is what can lead to feelings of uncertainty and anxiety, which negatively impacts our mental health.

Unfortunately, we live in a material world, and are often judged based on what we have. People can be financially crippled due to the fear of not having "enough" or wanting to appear to be "doing well" and will make significant financial decisions prematurely as a result, leaving them in an undesirable situation. For others, they may not be phased by the outsider's opinion on what they possess, rather just lack the knowledge on how best to manage their money. This can also land you in an equally undesirable position, with the same knock-on effects as previously discussed.

Flow State Money is about taking the principle of being in a 'Flow State', popularised by psychologists Csikszentmihalyi and Nakamura, and applying that concept to your relationship with money. As a result of that, your quality of life improves, along with your mindset - being in a state of complete certainty, with considerably less worry, and an ability to spend money with a clear conscience and feel good about it. By knowing and understanding how to manage your money as soon as pay day arrives, you are rewarded with a sense of clarity on your finances, once you have taken the necessary actions set out in this book you then know that the money you have allocated yourself to spend, is exactly for that, spending. This way you can spend your money and feel good about it, as opposed to the notorious feelings of guilt and regret nagging away in your mind.

What does it actually mean to be in a 'Flow State'?

"An optimal state of consciousness where we feel our best & we perform at our best"

"True engagement"

"Complete immersion"

> *"You may have experienced a Flow State at some point – that sense of fluidity between your body and your mind, where you are absorbed by and deeply focused on something, beyond the point of distraction. Time feels like*

it has slowed down. Your senses are heightened. You are at one with the task at hand, as action and awareness sync to create an effortless momentum. Some people describe this feeling as being 'in the zone'. This is the flow state and is accessible to everyone, whether you're engaged in a physical activity, a creative, or even a simple day to day task."

-HEADSPACE

Many of the above phrases give weight to the same ideas when applied to money. For instance, "fluidity between body and mind" corresponds with the same feeling experienced when you achieve a Flow State with your money. The difference being the fluidity is between yourself and your money. This means having complete certainty on what the purpose is for each pound you make and knowing exactly how you intend to manage it. Through taking this approach consistently, the good habits you implement will amplify this sense of fluidity. As you build upon these good habits, you will also build upon the "effortless momentum" described as you continue to get "in the zone" with your money. When in this position, it makes it infinitely easier to make smart decisions with your money, becoming more resistant to falling off track with your choices. From this deeper understanding, a sense of liberation and confidence with regards to your finances will become apparent and will continue to be the driving force behind the good decisions you make involving your finances.

When you are in a Flow State with your money, you reach complete focus and clarity on the direction of the issue that determines so many outcomes in our lives – money. As a result of this you begin to perform optimally in your general life as you drop those feelings of uncertainty that bring stress and anxiety. This very idea encapsulates the message of the book, and exactly where the title comes from as it completely underlines the concept itself.

Another way of looking at it

When it comes to financial management, we often hear people talking about ideas such as buying one less coffee a day and the impact it could have if it was invested and so on. This gives the impression that financial planning is all about frugality and watching every penny you spend. As much as I do think it is sensible to be mindful of your money, the frugal approach gives off a feeling of entrapment. I believe there is a more freeing way to approach finances, allowing you to live life and spend your hard-earned money guilt-free with enjoyment, whilst simultaneously securing your financial future.

The truth is that we cannot guarantee tomorrow, and we only get one go at this life!

So, how do we live life now and spend guilt free without always worrying about money, how does this tie into our lives overall and what would this mean for you as an individual? There are a few actionable steps that we must take to get there, and that's what I am going to share with you.

Through taking these steps you will be able to achieve "a Flow State with your money", allowing for peace of mind through incorporating Flow State into your life. In doing so you'll find it will heavily contribute towards becoming truly present in life, and at one with your finances.

WHO AM I?

I wrote this book with the purpose of trying to inspire others to make smart financial decisions, to help improve their overall life and financial well-being. Knowing and understanding some of the tools and strategies featured in this book, played a big part in transforming my life.

I truly hope you will find a message in this book that'll impact you in the same way it did for me. I'll be sharing knowledge and experience I've acquired through both my personal and professional life. This knowledge, accompanied by the actionable steps featured, will assist you in transforming your outlook on managing money, allowing you to secure and set a clear path for your future.

It is also important to note that the journey through which I gained my experience is something I'm confident many will empathise with. There is beauty within the struggle, and in sharing my story I believe it will make clear to anyone reading, that getting on the road to financial security is something that is accessible. No matter your starting point. With that in mind, I feel it is important for me to share some of my personal story, with the intention of showing you where I've come from, and why I feel it is so important for me to write this for others.

The Fire Sparked

My name's Joseph Obeng (formerly Hannam), and I think it's fair to say that I am not your typical financial adviser. I grew up in both Essex and North London, floating between my parents' homes. When I think back to my childhood, I have some amazing memories and many things to be thankful for. But with that also came struggles that we faced as a family. Overall, my life circumstances and the hardships encountered meant I had to grow up very quickly, and as a result - developing a specific mindset due to these experiences.

I lived with my mum, my three brothers, and my sister. We were the family on the street that people talked about and not in a good way. Constantly feeling judged because we were so different, and sometimes even assumed to be foster siblings due to said differences. Explaining the relations between us was tiresome. I am mixed-race (black African Ghanaian and white English), my younger brother and sister are white (Irish and English), and then my other brothers are mixed race (black West-indies & white English). We are related through our Mum - our English side. If you can make sense of all that I am impressed! So, from the outside looking in you would never know that we all had the same mum. Of course, we have different dads hence the reason for the variation in appearances. I suppose you can see why we stuck out so much.

I used to stay with my dad at the weekends and during the school holidays. I always enjoyed going to stay because I looked up to him a lot. My dad grew up in Tottenham, so he had a certain way about him. For anyone that knows about areas in Tottenham, you'll know that it takes a particular attitude to get through, and with that comes an inspiring story I think he should share one day.

My mum and dad had me when they were only seventeen years old and were separated before I was born. Being both children and separated parents bringing up a child, you can imagine my upbringing was a little unconventional. After my dad, my mum's choice in men was not always great, and played a big role in the problems found in our home. I experienced a lot of domestic violence growing up, alongside other unsavoury things a child shouldn't have to see.

My youngest brother on my Mum's side was born with a disability called cerebral palsy, the levels of this disability can vary, but his disability was of the severest form. It was an intense living situation and our Mum found this particularly difficult to deal with, and of course she needed help. As a result, a lot of the time many of the responsibilities used to fall on us siblings. As the oldest brother, I naturally adopted the role of the father figure in the family, which felt like a lot of pressure to take on. Also, a huge credit is owed to my brother one down from me who stepped up at a particularly young age to take on a huge amount of the responsibility of the care for our disabled brother, Kobe. As hard as our mum tried, she had a hard time coping with it all and understandably she struggled a lot with her mental wellbeing. Sometimes things would be great – despite everything we were dealing with. Most of the other times we would find ourselves in extremely challenging and difficult situations that I can only describe as emotionally traumatic.

To make matters more difficult, the state of our home was far from ideal. I was so embarrassed, that I would not let most of my school friends knock for me, choosing to meet them at the top of the road instead. It got to a point that I even remember hearing comments from our extended family members calling us tramps. It was deeply upsetting and very hard to deal with as a child.

Trying to navigate my way through this world amongst these circumstances, whilst understanding who I actually am, was very difficult and I often felt lost.

There was a particular moment during this period that really stuck with me! I had overheard a story that one of the school mum's, had said I was just going to be another f**k up, who'd be going nowhere in life... I assume this comment was made because of the living circumstances I was in at the time and the way people perceived us. Regardless of her reasoning I can't begin to explain how upsetting those words were to me, it hurt to hear that this was what people thought of me. This was one of the moments where I think things really changed in my mind and something happened inside me that day. A fire sparked, and all I wanted to do was prove these people wrong! As the great Les Brown says, "Don't let someone else's opinion of you become your reality". The only thing in my head after that instance, was to aspire to do better for myself and find a way to improve things for me and my family.

The Bottom of the Pit

At the time, the people around me that seemed to be doing well were all tradesmen of some sort. As a result, that's what I ended up working towards. I wanted money quickly, to try and show that I was doing well. At the time, like many people, I thought that just meant having money and nice things. Money wasn't coming fast enough, and I ended up accumulating a sizeable debt, possibly the biggest mistake I've made. Finding myself at the start of a difficult financial situation, I quickly found myself struggling and was at a loss for what to do.

During this time, there was a lot of stuff going on with my family and without going into detail, it was having a huge impact on me. It got to a point where I just felt like everything was crumbling down around me. I had lost relationships that were very important to me, and I was feeling like I didn't really have anyone to turn to. It was strange, because although there were so many people around me, I felt completely alone.

I found myself in a position where I felt like I struggled to fit in anywhere, which was increased tenfold by this new complex family dynamic. Seeming to be at the centre of all these intense and deep family problems (that honestly, I would need to write another book about to explain), I had lost some of my most important relationships, on top of having this 'big' debt looming over me. Inevitably, I was completely overwhelmed, sick with worry, and I found myself at breaking point.

I realised I'd hit the bottom of the pit and something had to change, immediately.

Internal Shift

The first thing I decided is that I wouldn't care about fitting in anymore. I was sick of always trying to blend in somewhere and the feeling of needing to be a part of something. I came to the conclusion that I was going to be the start of something new, creating my own 'thing' to be a part of.

I started to think deeply about what I really wanted out of life, and I found myself soul-searching. I then found this incredible personal development programme which helped me to start thinking differently and things started to turn around. The programme also led me to start learning about money. Exploring how to manage it and how to make it work for me. I was so inspired by this that before I knew it, I had read 3 or 4 different books on the topic. I started to put some of the processes in place, and for the first time ever I had this unbelievable sense of control over my life and this feeling of freedom (bearing in my mind I was still in debt at this stage). I knew that I still had a long way to go, but just that feeling of knowing exactly what I needed to do and what steps to take was a turning point for me. I started taking action and implementing the steps immediately. I think this was really the beginning of an internal shift and I started to see everything in a different light.

During this soul search, I came to the conclusion that I needed to interact with different types of people that complemented the new mind-set that I was starting to develop. I was also in a position where I needed to start making some money, but I wanted to aspire to becoming something I believed would never be possible for me. I wanted to defy the odds and show that I was more than just another 'f**k up'. But I had to take it further than that – I felt I needed to do something special that I could really feel proud of. Most importantly I just wanted to be a good role model for my younger brothers and sister and show them that we can all be more than what people perceived of us.

I'd heard some stories about working as a broker in the city and the drive it required. I also heard about the level of money you could earn if you were skilled at it. This really appealed to me, by putting me outside of my comfort zone, and being surrounded by motivated people, with the incentive of earning a great level of money. It seemed the perfect plan for achieving my original objective.

Unrealistic Ambition?

I set out on a mission to try and get some sort of position or internship as a junior broker – even if it meant I was just making tea for the first year. I just wanted to get myself in the industry so I could begin to grow. I asked a few friends if they had any contacts that could potentially help my plan, but I had no luck. The majority of job adverts posted required some form of previous experience and in many cases required certain qualifications. I didn't have either of those, but what I lacked in credentials I made up for in an excellent work ethic and burning desire to do well. The few places that I did contact rejected me swiftly. It began to feel as though this could be an unrealistic ambition, I was disheartened to say the least.

I found myself at the barbers one day and bumped into a guy I'd known from my school years. Being a little older than me, we had different friendship circles, but we got on well, and to my surprise he mentioned he was a broker in the city. Of course, I had to mention how tough I'd been finding it to try and get an opportunity as a junior/trainee broker and asked him if there was anything he could do to assist me. I was surprised at how willing he was to help, and he set me up a telephone interview with the recruiters at his workplace.

I couldn't believe how lucky I was, but then it dawned on me that I had to go through the telephone interview. I began to panic about all the questions they might ask me – in truth I knew nothing about this role – I just needed an opportunity to prove that I would do whatever it takes. The individual who had set up the telephone interview for me just said to be myself. I couldn't escape the thought of coming across as rough kid with a messed-up background and nothing to offer. As a result, I tried to research the markets so it could sound like I knew what I was talking about.

The day of the interview arrived, and I was anxiously pacing around, sweating with nerves. I had built it up so much in my head. Soon after, the phone rang. We quickly exchanged the pleasantries found at the beginning of most phone calls, then from there, everything declined. I started stuttering, my nerves were apparent in my voice and the more I became aware of how much I was struggling, the worse it got. The call didn't last very long but it felt like an hour. I knew as soon the call was over, I had completely messed it up. I became a wreck and just wanted the ground to swallow me up, I was humiliated. It felt like I had missed my big opportunity and that I probably wouldn't get another chance like it again.

After a few days of feeling sorry for myself, I decided that I couldn't give up because of one bad phone call – even if it was uncomfortable for me. I decided to start asking around again, and it became apparent to me that it might be a beneficial to get some sales experience as it was mentioned previously that brokers were just 'glorified salesman'. This made no sense to me at the time, but with my understanding of things now, it's quite an apt way of putting it. I thought if I can get a telesales job selling something, at least I would have some experience on the phone. I managed to get a job selling double glazing and windows. It turns out that finding decent people to sell windows and doors isn't at all easy and they gladly took me on.

When I walked in on my first day, I felt like a complete idiot. Most people were younger than me, even the manager of the team was younger than me. I couldn't help but ask myself what the hell I was doing there – I could quickly tell that you didn't have do much to get this job and it suddenly felt like another low point in my life. However, what these people didn't know was the reason that I was actually there, to get some experience on the phone, cold calling, dealing with objections and persevering to produce results. I had far bigger ambitions and this was simply a means to an end. I was sure that if I could prove to myself that I can do this here then I at least know that I can handle the phone. Apparently, this was considered to be the most gruelling part of being a junior broker, so I had to do it. I thought if I can do that, then surely someone would hire me.

I had done the telesales job for about two months and found that after a little practice and building my confidence, I was actually quite good on the phone. I only had a few shifts a week doing telesales, so to earn some additional money, I decided set-up an event with a couple of friends. We used to run a night in some bars in Essex, and we were fairly successful. This worked well for me, because it was only ever on a Friday or Saturday night, and we would promote over social media during the week. On top of this, I was also doing some part-time work as a waiter at the West Ham football ground. I worked in the Chairman's suite which was a cool experience! As you can tell I was doing whatever I could to acquire some money, whilst pursuing my main goal I had set.

Still eager to land a position as a junior broker, one day on the train home from a shift at West Ham, there were two young guys sitting opposite me, they were wearing slick suits and Rolexes - they looked like brokers to me. I don't know what came over me but out of nowhere, without a second thought, I just approached one of the guys and said, "do you work as a broker by any chance?" and he looked at me, surprised, seemingly on edge, I think he thought he was about to get mugged! He nervously replied, "Yeah I do, why's that?", I explained that I had been attempting to get a role as a junior broker and asked him if he could give me any pointers on how to go about it. He said to me "purely for the fact that you just had the guts to come over and start speaking to me like that, I'd happily interview you for a role on my desk at the firm I work". He gave me his details and said come for an interview 10am the next morning and to call him once I got to Canary Wharf. We were on the Central Line and the stops are quick and often, so the conversation was a short one. I only got his name, mobile number, and the name of the firm.

I couldn't believe my luck. I left the train in complete disbelief – it felt like that was the type of thing you only you see in a film.

I was so pleased with myself, the fact that I had the courage to do that, but I think I was driven by wanting it so badly. Having already been rejected and failing numerous times in my previous attempts, I thought one more rejection really wasn't going to bother me that much. To my surprise it paid off! I learnt a valuable lesson that day: sometimes, it's best to not think and just do! I have no doubt that if I had started thinking into it, I would have talked myself out of it.

Breakthrough!

I arrived at Canary Wharf at 9am the next morning, just to make sure I was on time. I gave him a call as he suggested to get the directions to the office, but there was no answer. After several times of trying to get through, I was starting to feel like I had been strung along – and was trying to convince myself it couldn't be true. I only had 10 minutes before the time he had arranged for the interview and still couldn't get through to him.

Standing outside Canary Wharf station feeling like a fool in my unfitting suit, wearing an old pair of shoes that I had tried to polish up, and lost. I decided I would approach some people and ask if they knew where this particular place was. I had no luck and found myself sitting around hoping to get a call back, but I quickly came to the realisation the call wasn't coming...

At this point I was standing around near one of the bars by the station, wondering what to do, I saw these other two guys, again, dressed up smartly, one was just laughing away. I overheard him say something like, "it's not even 10 in the morning and I've already banked 8 grand", that caught my attention. I was thinking maybe these two could help me, they definitely looked like brokers too. Once again without a second thought, I marched straight up to them and just asked if they knew where this place was, both looked me up and down and just replied, "nah sorry mate". Then one of them asked me why I was looking for the building, and so I told them my situation. He then asked, "An interview for what?" I replied, "A junior broker role." to which he cockily responded, "I run a desk at a currency brokerage come and work for me." I assume he was just in a great mood from the deal he'd made that morning. I took them by surprise and asked to begin the interview now, whilst sitting down at their table. Amused, they began to laugh. I couldn't tell whether he was just messing with me or not, but he turned to me and replied, "Alright, fair enough". He asked me a few questions, and as he was finishing up his drink, he invited me to their offices. Obviously, I jumped at the opportunity, and I'll never forget the feeling as we went into the inside, getting into the lift to the 32nd floor of the Citibank building in Canary Wharf.

To many people this probably isn't a big deal, but from where I was coming from, I couldn't believe what was happening. He showed me around the office, filled with suited up young guys on their phones, in front of their double screened computers. The atmosphere was insane. He asked me a few more questions and concluded that he liked my enthusiasm and asked when I could start. I said I could start as soon as possible, and that was it - I finally had a breakthrough!

Back in the pit

To begin with I was on top of the world! The pay there as a junior on the desk was abysmal, but at the time, I was naïve, and ultimately grateful that I had managed to land a position. I didn't even care about the money.

However, after around 2 months of working there, it was already starting to feel like I was driving myself into the ground. This was due to the abysmal pay and being belittled, all within ridiculous hours. As I discussed before, from what I learnt about money, a key rule of managing it is spending less than you earn, and when I totalled my living expenses, with eating and travel, I was negative every month. It felt as though I was consistently driving myself into a hole. The ridiculously long hours meant I was unable to fit anything else in to subsidise the appalling amount I was earning at the time. I could barely keep the promoting going for the club nights at the weekends. Although the prospect of transitioning from junior broker to broker was still appealing, I felt as though I was going backwards.

I had started to feel like perhaps I was sold a dream with this company, and it didn't seem like there was really much chance of moving up at all. However, I persevered, and told myself I was still just starting out. On one occasion, I was called into a meeting with several other members of the team, and we were all fired on the spot. I was speechless. I was hitting all my targets despite only being there two months. I got heated and something took over me, I spoke out and I made it clear in no uncertain terms exactly what I thought. I couldn't accept it. They had me burning myself out for the last two months, for what felt like absolutely nothing.

Somehow, my outburst kept me the job, with the head of the desk suddenly seeming to have a newfound respect for me. I was sick of feeling like life was always getting the better of me. From then on, I was treated quite differently, and nobody spoke down to me anymore. My pay still didn't go up unfortunately. I noticed over time that employee turnover was high and realised that though it was brilliant for me in terms of experience, I was not going to get very far. After all the effort I had gone to in getting to that position. It appeared this was not quite the right direction for me.

A little experience pays off

After a few more months, I used my experience to try and land another role elsewhere. Eventually securing a role at a currency brokerage in Central London. It was a much better organisation and I felt I was able to grow there. I stayed at this company for three years. During my time there, my desire to do well was still strong, and I managed to work my way up to heading a small team and a Senior Broker role. I felt incredibly proud of myself for finally getting to this position, I was working with driven people and many of them with a similar mind-set. By this point I had already surpassed my doubters' expectations of me by far.

I was well on track with sorting my money problems and clearing all my debts, committed to the lessons that I had learnt - many that I am going to share with you. Despite everything I went through to get there, it was all worth it, because it helped get me this role – it goes to show a little experience pays-off.

Something was missing

Surprisingly, I had lost interest in the role quickly and I realised it was not what I thought I wanted. It felt like something still wasn't quite right.

I found myself returning to the personal development programme that I found some years before. It led me to deeper thinking again and it dawned on me that I really wasn't doing something that I enjoyed. Although the journey was beneficial for me up until that point – I was getting very little fulfilment from what I was doing. I felt complacent. I needed to put myself in an uncomfortable position again to help me grow further, which meant I needed something new and bigger to challenge myself with. I still had this constant thought in my mind to achieve something I never thought possible for me.

With everything I had managed to accomplish so far, it was like I was fearful each time I was stepping into the unknown with this built-up picture in my mind of this great 'thing' I was after. But each time I got there I felt disappointed, and I was coming to realise that there was a lot more to me and this journey than I previously knew.

Never thought this would be possible for me

I had been attending business networking events, where I happened to meet a now good friend of mine who is a financial planner. After a few months of learning about what he does, it appeared to be something I would enjoy doing. There were many elements to this role that just felt like they were made for me, but it wasn't going to be a case of just being bold and approaching strangers this time. You must be FCA authorised for this role, which meant a lot of exams and getting qualifications – for those of you that don't know, the FCA (Financial Conduct Authority) are the regulators of the financial sector.

It was a while before we spoke about the potential of me becoming a financial planner for the firm that he worked at. However, when we did, he believed I had all the right attributes for the role. I think those words were enough to help me to take a leap of faith. He said there was a position coming up that he would happily recommend me as someone to take on.

After my interview, I realised the magnitude of the company that I would be representing and what the importance of my new role would be. I quickly realised that this was the something I was looking for.

Before I knew it, I had left my job and started a new role as a trainee financial planner. This meant taking a big pay cut, I would not be able to earn any real money until I had passed the exams, I had a lot of work to do. There are 6 external exams, and for each of them the study books were like A4 sized bibles, and then there were several internal exams too. The last time I done any real exams were my GCSE's and though I had performed quite well on them, it was 10 years ago, I was 26 at this point, so it had been a decade since I'd sat an exam. Plus, they were on a completely different level and would be the hardest thing I would have to overcome so far.

I was determined to make this happen and started studying to get these qualifications to become a financial planner as soon as I could. I had heard of instances where people were taking years to pass the exams, but I had just taken a big pay cut and had responsibilities to take care of. For that reason, I needed a game plan to complete it sooner than a couple of years! I aimed to get it done in one year, as this would to help build momentum towards getting my qualifications.

I studied relentlessly day and night; I struggled immensely to get through the first exam. I then really struggled to get through the second exam. I was starting to feel like I had made a big mistake, I still had 5 exams to get through. It quickly seemed like an impossible task, and I did consider giving up. However, I knew how disappointed I'd be with myself if I gave up and I felt I still had more to give. Passing became something I had to do to prove myself, and so I continued studying, sacrificing any kind of social life for my career. This laser focus kicked in and after just over one year, I managed to pass all the exams, and became a qualified financial planner for the one of the biggest financial advisory firms in the UK.

Of course, I wasn't ready to go out and start advising straight away. After some further training and shadowing some of the senior advisers, I was out on my own advising clients on their investments and financial planning for the future. With some time, I was acquiring clients that were investment bankers from the likes of J.P. Morgan, Barclays Investment Bank, and even Partners from law firms – I couldn't comprehend the progress I'd made.

Getting to this point probably doesn't seem like a big deal to some people, however the journey that I had to get to this point meant that this was a truly significant point in my life. The fact that these clients with important positions and high paid jobs, were taking my advice was something I never thought would be possible for someone like me.

What I loved so much about it, was that it took everything that I had learned about money in the personal-development programme to another level and I found myself just constantly working on it and developing my new craft.

In my first full calendar year as an appointed qualified financial adviser, I made 'partner' level. I was making good money and going on some amazing trips. I still remember the feeling when I had my first ever client who decided to invest £1 million with me - I couldn't ever imagine this happening to me. The whole time I was just reminded how people used to think I'm just a 'rough kid with a messed-up background'. But that was the thing, I was no longer letting my past define me. I had been on a journey and grown so far from that young boy. I was now a fully qualified, FCA authorised financial planner for one of the biggest financial advisory firms in the UK. It seemed like suddenly people were looking at me differently and treating me differently too. For me personally, it was honestly astonishing how far I'd managed to come, considering my life before.

Inner-Breakthrough!

Still, somehow, after achieving all of this, I woke up one day feeling deflated with a feeling of something still lacking in my career. I couldn't quite put my finger on it, but I think a lot of this came from having to act in a particular way to fit in. This was frustrating as I had previously vowed to stop attempting to appease others by fitting into their idea of how I should be. This profession is made up of a demographic that is the complete opposite end of the scale to mine. You don't see many people that look like me working in my role, although I do feel like that is starting to change. On top of that, I come from a world that most of the people in this profession just simply wouldn't understand. Being in the minority of people in this industry who haven't been to university was difficult, constantly feeling like I had to justify myself for others had me feeling like I had to hide my true self. This had me struggling to truly connect with people.

Because of this feeling, I felt obligated to share my story with others who could empathise with my background and ambitions. I have managed to gain a wealth of knowledge and experience that could help many people, from all backgrounds with varying qualities of life. Coming from a tough background myself, I'd like to share my newfound knowledge with others, whilst showing it is absolutely possible to exceed people's expectations of you.

I found my passion for helping others through a conversation I'd had with someone close to me. I could tell something was up and felt the urge to invite them over to speak properly. My goal from the conversation was to make sure they felt much better when they were leaving than how they felt when we first spoke. Throughout the conversation, it transpired that a key factor that had them feeling down was the debt they had accumulated, and the lack of control they had over their finances. This had left them feeling like they had no real control over what was happening in their life at the time.

I went through things with them step by step and helped them see things differently. The main thing was that I helped them to understand how to manage the money situation as well as the other things going on in their life. After we had finished chatting, they said "thank you man", and came over and gave me a big hug. When they left, they were smiling and joking, and said "I feel like I know what to do now", which was incredible to hear. It was such an amazing feeling to know that by sharing some of these things that I'd learnt, I was able to have a big impact on someone else's life. That's when it hit me, I realised this was something that gave my life deeper meaning and perhaps this was something I was meant to be doing. I've always found joy in helping people, but this way I can make a difference in people's lives. This was the inner breakthrough for me and though I'd been on this whole journey to get to this point, I think it was something I had to do to realise this sense of purpose.

I started doing some research with an anonymous survey on a range of different people from different backgrounds, in a variety of different income brackets. I concluded that 80% of people have anxiety issues when it comes to money and their personal finances, and many even said they felt embarrassed. The crazy thing is that in so many cases people who would be considered by most to have a great income still found themselves having major problems around money. This came as a surprise to me because I was expecting it to exclusively be the people in the lower income brackets. I suppose people aren't usually that open about their true situation with money, but with this being an anonymous survey, they were comfortable to be more open with the truth.

The number one issue that arose from my research about money was the stress that it has on many couple relationships and marriages. My research determined that people would benefit from lessons and a better knowledge of how to manage money. Whether that's debt repayment, financial protection, savings, and investments, or just how to structure it. My results also showed that people said they would happily pay for a short course to help resolve any problems in this area of their life.

I started to think how amazing it would be if I was able to help people change their lives for the better with my lessons – regardless of who they are or how much money they earn. Mental health and well-being are spoken about so much in the current climate, and one of the biggest things that impact our anxiety and stress levels is money and the responsibility around it. I must highlight, it is not that having more money is going to take away all stress and anxiety. It is about understanding that money is a tool that helps facilitate so many things that we love doing, that bring us happiness and can heavily impact how we feel. Consequently, management of that tool is imperative.

I continued to work for the financial planning firm for five years in total, and with that came fantastic knowledge and experience. I then took another leap of faith and I have now set up my own Financial Planning business. I advise on investments and future financial planning for individuals and small businesses. We help them to build the financial grounding and structure for generating & managing wealth as well as structure their finances and investments tax-efficiently.

In my profession, people always talk about how every person should have financial advice. However, the level of time and work required, in comparison to the reward, means it only appears to be worthwhile for the financial planner if the client has a sizeable salary as well as disposable income and a large lump sum to invest. This means that there is a huge number of the population that simply will not get the financial advice or guidance they need, because it will either be far too costly for them or far too costly for the financial planner – someone loses out either way.

Therefore, this book is an attempt to help try and fill that void and to give some guidance to anyone that finds it useful. Particularly those people who perhaps aren't quite earning incomes as high as mentioned above, or even far lower than that. This book is also aimed at people that find themselves in a difficult situation with money like I did, or perhaps find it all a bit overwhelming. I felt that by sharing these ideas and this knowledge with you, at least you can get your financial grounding set up and understand how to start building a secure financial future as well still live your life now.

As a personal project beside my business, 'Flow State Money' is the beginning of me creating something for others to be a part of. Building your financial grounding, regardless of how much money you earn is the key to financial success and to support the life you want. This allows you to enjoy life now as well as secure your financial future. Helping you understand exactly what to do with your money the moment each payday arrives will give you a liberating feeling of freedom and control. I plan to bring you a short video series as a follow up from this book, but this book will be the start and is the perfect place to get things kicked-off! It brings me great joy to share this knowledge and information with you. I know that once you implement this into your own personal lives it will have a powerful and life-changing impact. Let's begin.

F irstly, I want to begin with discussing some of the common misconceptions around money.

Misconception 1
Making more money will make you more rich

Most people think their problem with money stems from how much they earn, but the truth is - they have a money management problem as well as a problem with their relationship with money. Attempting to earn more money might help, but it is often not the solution to your money problems. If you do not change your money habits, and just increase your income, you usually just end up with bigger money problems! You must change the way you manage money and your habits to overcome your money problems.

Misconception 2
What the word 'Wealth' means

To have wealth or to be wealthy is to have an abundance of valuable financial assets or money, but abundance means different things to different people. When people think of the word wealth, they tend to think of people with Bentleys, Rolexes, and yachts. Many people think this is unrealistic for them, so they are put off, and immediately reject the idea of having or building wealth. However, you do not necessarily need to have these things to be 'what many class as wealthy', because it is all relative to the individual and the lifestyle they desire. Many people have no interest in having the material things or they're happy with less eccentric material things – so just because an individual has fewer financial assets it doesn't necessarily mean they are less wealthy. It is all relative. In simpler terms, if a person has enough 'wealth' or resources to sustain the lifestyle they wish to lead, without having to exchange their time for money, then that person, by definition, is wealthy. For that reason, it is crucial to not be intimidated by the word wealth and rule yourself out as someone that can be wealthy or build wealth over time.

Misconception 3
That investing is only for the rich

I've had many conversations where people say to me that they don't earn enough money to invest. It is very clear to me that many people believe you need considerable lump sums to invest to make it worthwhile, but that is simply not true. Investing is a journey and the earlier you get started the better, regardless of how much you are investing to begin with – this will become apparent throughout the book.

Misconception 4
If I don't have enough money when I'm old, The
Government will look after me

To be completely blunt, I wouldn't rely on this personally.

Misconception 5
I'll win the lottery or meet someone rich!

I put this in here partly joking, but there are definitely some believers in this misconception. I have come across many people with this blasé attitude, thinking that something (or someone) will just fall out of the sky, solving everything, until reality hits and it's too late. There's too much at stake to rely on an approach that probably won't materialise, and that price is usually regret and hardship. It would be foolish to rely on this.

BUILDING BLOCKS OF
FINANCIAL PLANNING

This book is structured based upon the building blocks of financial planning shown on the next pages. Each chapter represents a building block, going in order. Reading the steps in this structured way should make it easy to understand. Follow the steps as you go through each chapter it will all be worth it. If you do not have any debt, you do not need to worry about 'Building Block X', though it could still be beneficial, and perhaps you could help somebody you know.

As the diagrams show on the next pages, you wouldn't build your proverbial house on sand. You need a good solid grounding to start building your wealth on, and the building blocks shared in the next chapters are the building blocks to give you this foundation.

<u>Building blocks if you are debt free</u>

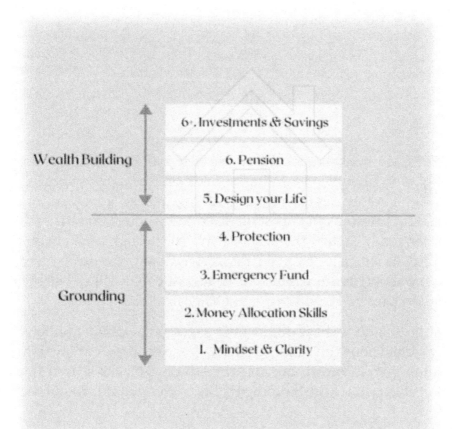

Diagram 1

Building blocks if you have debts

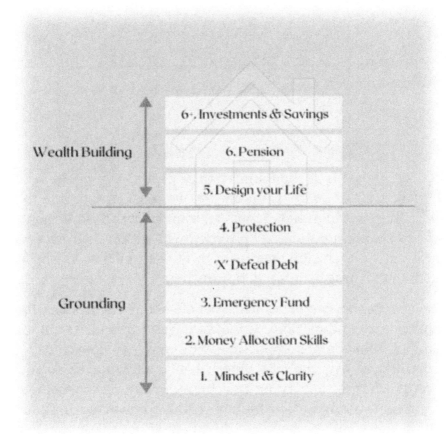

Diagram 2

BUILDING BLOCK 1 – MINDSET & CLARITY

Mindset is at the foundation of everything we do. Before we can do anything in life, we must first decide to do it in our mind. However, a lot of what we decide we can and cannot do is already programmed within us from a very young age, so over a long period of time, they will become beliefs, and many of these beliefs will be limiting.

When someone has a 'limiting belief' about themselves for a significant period of time, it makes it very difficult to undo or change it, but it's not impossible. The more we consciously do something, it can soon become a habit, allowing us to move towards what we are trying to achieve. In this case becoming a person that manages their money well. Before we tackle this, we must decide what new belief we might like to have about ourselves to help change our habits and behaviours with money, which will be further discussed later.

<u>Common Limiting Beliefs</u>

"Having lots of money is greedy"

"Having too much money will make you unhappy"

"Money is the route to all evil"

"If you make too much money you won't know who your real friends are"

"Money doesn't grow on trees"

"Everyone will just want something from you if you have too much money"

"Why make more money if I just have to pay more tax"

"Having a lot of money is too much responsibility and hassle"

These are just some of the common things we hear growing up that might lead to these limiting beliefs. Having these thoughts and ideas around money built into us can have a huge impact on our behaviour with money and therefore must be considered in this process.

As the Author, Morgan Housel, describes in his book the 'The Psychology of Money' - "Doing well with money has little to do with how smart you are and a lot to do with how you behave".

Morgan also states that - "Financial success is not a hard science, it's a soft skill. How you behave is just as important, if not more important than what you know".

There's a couple of books that I feel cover the topic of behaviour around money really well, and I would encourage you to read them if you would like to discover more about money behaviours.

The Psychology of Money by Morgan Housel

Money Mindset by Elena G. Rivers

The first thing we should look to do is change some of these beliefs that we might have around money to be more positive. For example you could think about all the good you can do and the positive differences you could make.

Money is neither good nor bad. It is simply just money, it's an object.

It is only the decisons made by people because of money or with money, or their view on money that can be determined as good or bad. So, the decision is really yours.

It is also important to understand that your reasons for wanting to obtain and manage money well, are stronger than the object of money itself. What I mean by that is, if you have specific reasons why you are becoming a person that is great at managing money, (other than the fact that it will have a hugely positive impact on your life), it makes it much easier to stay on track with it. For example, you might want to worry less, so that your mood improves, leading to a better relationship with your family. Perhaps you want to ensure that your children have the life that you wish you had growing up and give them a better start. Whatever they might be – just remember that 'your reasons why' are more important than money itself. Managing your money without understanding why, might lead to procrastination or just not even doing it at all. With that being said, good methods for setting out goals will be discussed at length in a following chapter, and I would say this is possibly one of the most important points to take away from this book.

People are often unaware that they need to work on their finances until they do a financial health-check, to then discover what their finances actually mean for them over their lifetime. Therefore, even if you feel as though you are good with your finances, it is still beneficial to run through the steps and establish how on track you really are.

Lessons from the past

"The past is a school, not a social club. So,
learn from it, don't hang out there."

- *Jim Rohn*

The first step that needs to be tackled, is getting to the root of how our relationship with money developed.

To really make a change, the first tool needed is awareness and the next is action. Consequently, our awareness will need to be explored, to get a better understanding of ourselves when it comes to our relationship with money. Usually that means a period of reflection.

Our relationship with money is generally built on the foundations of our earliest experiences and lessons around it. The funny thing is, as children, we tend to learn the most when we are not being taught. We pick up habits and ideologies from our environment, subconsciously, without realising. Therefore, it's likely that your relationship with your money and the habits that emerge will have already developed long before you have any money of your own to deal with and manage.

This usually means the majority of what we have learned about money comes from the people who raised us or grew up with. Parents, grandparents, carers, older siblings to name a few. The problem with this is that most people have poor money management skills, and in most cases that's what has been passed down to us. It is also true that many people will be quite disciplined with their money, but then lack a true understanding of money itself, meaning they're not managing it in an optimal way.

It is important to consider how we came to be where we are today, personally as well as financially. This will allow us to reach an understanding on how our money habits were formed, allowing us to identify our strengths and acknowledge our weaknesses. By understanding ourselves better, it will make it much easier to make the right financial decisions going forward. We can then start to build a framework that allows us to be able to live life freely whilst doing the things we want to without the feeling of guilt when spending money. It comes down to your money habits, your thoughts, your feelings, and attitude towards money.

To get you thinking and perhaps learn a bit more about your relationship with money, please answer the following questions. You can either just have a think about them or write them down. I would suggest noting it down so you can refer back to it.

1. What is your earliest memory of something that you feel influenced how you think about money?

2. What was the attitude around money in the environment you grew up in?

A worksheet has been created for you to be able to keep this all neatly in one place. There's a couple of tasks in the book and the worksheet is avilable to support the process.

You can a get copy of the Flow State Money Workseet if you email 'FSM WORKSHEET' to:

contact@flowstatemoney.co.uk

FLOW-STATE-MONEY

WORKSHEET

Understanding the present

Now that we have a good idea of where our habits and attitude towards money has come from, let's think about how our financial situation looks right now...

Then think about what we would really like our financial situation to look like - I'm sure that for the vast majority of us, those two pictures look very different.

So, this is the part where we start to action and start the beginnings of our change.

The best way to get a clear picture of how things look for you, is by making a list of all your assets (if any), things like cash, property etc. Then your debts (if any), mortgage, credit cards etc and subtract your debts from your assets. This will effectively give you your net worth.

Then make a list of all your sources of income, and minus your expenditure (monthly bills) and your discretionary expenditure (non-essentials). It is generally easier to use an average for discretionary, as this is likely to vary each month.

This is a fairly simple task and should just give you a clear picture of how things look now. It often leads to the discovery that your money habits need improvement if you're unhappy with how it looks.

It's helpful to do this on a spreadsheet and save it. If you are not experienced with using spreadsheets, you can just write it out instead. This will give you a clear view and the reality of your starting point.

The 'FSM Starter Spreadsheet' with a video demonstration on how to use it has been created for you to assist you in this important task.

You can a get copy of the 'FSM Starter Spreadsheet' if you email 'FSM STARTER SPREADSHEET' to:

contact@flowstatemoney.co.uk

New Money Attitude

To follow up, begin to think about the future and how you'd like to envision it. Ask yourself, what type of person do you want to be, financially speaking. It is important to understand that at this stage we are not thinking about the material aspects of the future, but rather the type of person we would like to be with regards to our finances.

A good way to think about it is, if you had to describe now, how you were with money, what would you say? Write all the words down that come to your mind. Then think about how you would ideally want to describe yourself with money and write down all the words that come to mind. Take 5 minutes to do this before moving on.

Now that you have a good understanding of the type of person you would like to be with your money, begin to think about the actions that could be taken to get from where you are now to the type of person that you have described. Some examples could be to get out of debt, save regularly, or spend more sensibly. This will vary a great deal for each person, as everyone will have their own unique set of circumstances. However, you define your own circumstances, make sure you write them down.

Now you will find yourself aware of exactly the type of person you want to be with your money, and the actions that you think you need to take. With this realised, you'll now have the opportunity to understand the actions you need to take to help you become the individual you visualised.

BUILDING BLOCK 2 -
FLOW STATE MONEY
ALLOCATION SKILLS

Money allocation skills are essential for financial success. If you struggle to master your money allocation skills, you will find it increasingly more difficult to progress with your finances.

Why this is key

The idea of money leaves many people in a state of uncertainty, worry or fear. As a result of these overwhelming feelings, inevitably people end up burying their head in the sand.

Using these money allocation skills will allow for clarity, and a greater understanding of your personal finances. This knowledge has the ability to bring a sense of freedom, because you are now fully understanding of your situation, thus in control.

Reaching this feeling of clarity and understanding means you can make financial decisions that affect your life with confidence, you can feel positive about the money you spend (or don't spend). This is a far more favourable position in comparison to the never-ending argument surrounding whether you can truly afford something, alongside the constant feeling of regret.

Taking the above into account, this ultimately gives you control over your life. The feeling of control will no doubt bring certainty and ease, having a positive impact on your general wellbeing and quality of life.

To a certain degree, it is not about the amount of money, it is about the plan with the money. Now, we have to think about that statement sensibly because of course if you desire a higher costing level of lifestyle, then the likelihood is that you 'will' need to be able to generate more money. But the point is that for many people they are earning enough money but still somehow feel like they never have any or still feel like they need more and that's usually because they are not managing their money effectively.

We hear these stories all the time about people who earn less and appear to be less wealthy on the face of it but manage their money well in the background. Then you get these people who appear 'wealthy' and earn more, but they have poor money management skills and on paper are far less wealthy than the lower earner. That's because of a lack of money allocation skills and understanding your personal finances properly.

It's not about being tight or being frugal - it's being real with yourself and living within your means. Once I've planned out my money and taken care of my responsibilities - I know exactly how much I've got to spend, and I spend it freely and happily because that's exactly what it's for - spending!

Every single £ you earn should be allocated a job so that your money is serving you!

For example, preparing for the future (paying yourself first), protecting yourself and your family, living life today, lifestyle costs, giving back etc...

We will discuss this more, further in the chapter.

Important Lessons

Have 2 current accounts

There are a multitude of ways to manage your current accounts. I am going to discuss a strategy that I know works very well alongside the method of financial planning I am sharing with you. I even use it myself.

Put simply, the method is to have one account that you use for your direct debits, and another account to be used as your spending account. Always leave enough in your direct debits account to cover them for the month, so that whatever you have transferred into your spending account is yours to spend. This technique enables you to spend within your limit each month, living within your means as a result. You should not carry the card for your direct debits account with you, as this defeats the purpose.

Pay yourself first

I was first introduced to the concept 'Pay yourself first' from the late motivational speaker, Jim Rohn. It is one of the most valuable lessons I have learnt and is one of the key secrets to building wealth.

If you find yourself in debt, then paying down the debt is classed as paying yourself first. This is due to the fact that even though the money is paid away, it is reducing your debt, and consequently increasing your net worth.

Once you are debt free, (or if you are already debt free) saving and investing is the way in which you are able to pay yourself first. A pension pot: or as I like to call a freedom fund, is usually the optimal place to start. This should be done before you focus on paying any bills or any other expenses. The first person that you should be paying is yourself. Most people are used to paying all their bills, spending some more money, and finally seeing what's left at the end of the month, potentially saving that amount. That simply will not work for building wealth over time. The way to build wealth over time is to pay yourself first, and then live life based on the means that you have available – this way you will be setting yourself up for financial success in the future.

With this idea in mind, the obvious question presents itself - what is the appropriate amount to pay yourself? This will differ depending on each individual, their lifestyle, and how early they would like to achieve financial freedom. However, as a suggestion, I would say a good start is at least 10% of your earnings. That's £1 out of every £10 that you earn, do you think you could save/invest that each pay day?

Many people will find it just as easy living on 90% of their income versus 100%, making it complete sense to pay yourself first. This will be further explored in Building Block Six.

Set this 10% to come out of your 'Direct Debits Account' as a direct debit so that you are paying yourself without having to physically do it yourself. This is vitally important as human nature tells us if you leave it up to yourself to do manually each month it probably won't happen. There is a great book written on this concept by David Bach called 'The Automatic Millionaire' I would encourage you to read it at some point.

Pay day plan and actions

This is where the money allocation skills are crucial, and this is a very important part of the process.

I have created a video demonstration of this explanation too, with a downloadable spreadsheet so you are able to start applying this lesson straight away. The content of the lesson is a little more in depth and therefore easier to grasp through the medium of a video.

To receive this, please email 'FSM PDPA' to:

contact@flowstatemoney.co.uk

BUILDING BLOCK 3 – YOUR FINANCIAL CUSHION (EMERGENCY FUND)

Introduction to emergency funds

Building an emergency fund is a huge step towards getting complete control. This is not only due to the peace of mind attained, but because of the new habits and behaviours nurtured in creating the emergency fund. It places you in a strong position for a greater chance of success when it comes to the wealth building part of money management.

Two types of emergency fund

The first thing to be understood is that there are two types of emergency fund:

1. The first type is for if you have debt

   • Starter Emergency Fund

2. The second type is for once you have managed to clear your debt or if you already are debt free.

   • Full Emergency Fund

How to think about emergency funds

This might seem obvious, but emergency funds are for emergencies only.

It is best to leave emergency funds in a separate instant access cash type account.

It would be fair to argue about high inflation and low interest rates, as a reason to not leave any money in cash. Whilst this is a very valid point, it is important to remember the purpose of the emergency fund. The function of the emergency fund is not to try and build wealth, its function is to build a solid grounding, on which to build wealth for the future whilst accommodating for emergencies.

If you are unsure on how high inflation rates and low interest rates affect cash, please see Diagram 4, I have put at the end of the chapter.

The emergency fund is amazing psychologically, for that sense of security & peace of mind.

When an emergency comes along, you will not have to depend on credit or borrowing money to cover the bill.

How much should it be?

Starter Emergency Fund:

£500 - £1000; or One month's worth of essential expenditure

Full Emergency Fund:

Three months of essential expenditure is the rule of thumb; however, some people favour having six months' worth. It is best to do whatever you feel most comfortable with, but between three and six months is usually a good amount.

How to start the emergency fund?

This is dependent on your surplus income and how much gets spent on things you don't need. Because of this there might be some short-term pain for long-term gain.

If you have a high amount of surplus income then it should be fairly easy to do, it's just a case of setting some money aside each month until the emergency fund is fully funded.

If you find you don't have a high amount of surplus income, then you might have to make some short-term sacrifices to get it done. Perhaps there's some things that you spend money that are not necessities, that you can cut back on for a short period until you've grown your emergency fund. Maybe you could see if there are things you have that you no longer use that you could sell, there are lots of apps that make this easy to do. Or perhaps you could find another way of making extra money, if necessary.

Where should you keep your emergency fund?

I favour the newer online accounts to hold an emergency fund, like Monzo for example. Personally, this works well for me, because you have the ability to create cash pots which is brilliant for when it comes to managing money effectively.

If you have one of the accounts that allow you to create cash pots, then you can just keep your emergency fund in a cash pot and label it 'Emergency Fund'.

If you do not have one of these types of accounts, then you should be able to set up a separate online e-saver type of account with your bank. You should do this to keep your emergency fund separate from your spending and direct debits account(s). However, setting up new accounts can have an impact on your credit score so you should consider this before setting up a new account.

The main thing is that it is kept separate, in an instant access cash account.

When to dip into the emergency fund & what happens when you do.

As we have established, the emergency fund for emergencies only. So, the first question you should ask yourself when an 'emergency' comes up, is - Can I pay for this emergency out of my normal income?

Depending on whether you are at the stage of paying off debt, or at the stage of saving & investing (building wealth), it will differ on what to do when you must dip into your emergency fund:

If you're at the stage of paying down debt:

If you have had to use some, or all of your emergency fund, you should consider it a debt to yourself. Which means you should pay this back as priority over credit cards and loans. That does not mean stopping payments to your credits and loans, all it means is reverting to minimum payments on your credit card and loans. And making topping up the emergency fund your priority. This may seem abnormal, but it is important for you to have this peace of mind fund, to prevent you from taking out any further debts in the future.

If you're at the stage of saving & investing:

In most cases you'll be doing one of two things, or both. Paying into a pension or/and paying into an ISA (ideally an investment ISA, but we'll talk more about this later). If you're paying into a pension then try your best to keep that going because as it stands, the pension is currently the most tax-efficient way to build wealth. If you're paying into an ISA, then stop that and re-direct it to your emergency fund until you are back up to your required amount and then re-direct it back into the ISA.

Put simply into steps

1. Starter emergency fund (if you are at the stage where you need to pay down debts)

2. Pay down debts

3. Funded emergency fund (Once all debts are cleared)

Having this is in place alone will feel like a huge achievement, especially if you are coming from a place of having to pay down debts initially. It is massively valuable just purely for your mind, and you will get a sense huge relief getting to this point as you are now ready start building wealth (saving & investing).

4. Ready to start building wealth

This diagram shows how the rise in the cost of living (inflation growth) can outweigh the interest you get in your bank account. Therefore, reducing the real value of your money held in the bank.

Diagram 4.

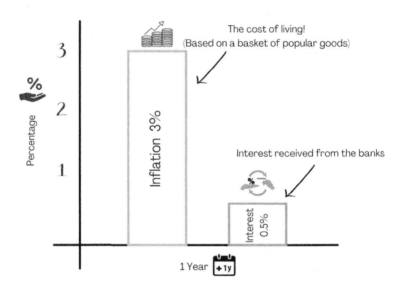

If the cost of living (inflation) is going up by 3% per year but the interest you receive from the banks is only 0.5%, then you are effectively losing 2.5% per year on the value of your cash in the bank. *These figures used are just as examples for the illustration and we will vary from year to year.*

BUILDING BLOCK 'X' - DEFEAT DEBT

I f there's one thing that will inhibit your potential to be financially secure, it's debt! The trap of debt can be hard to get out of, and often people find themselves in debt for a large portion of their lives if they don't take action to sort it properly. What gets people into to debt is poor habits, but to get out of debt you have to break these habits. Financially secure people don't deal with bad debt. It becomes a heavy weight on your shoulders that you carry around with you and for many people, over time that weight gets heavier and heavier, unless they change their habits.

You'll recount from my personal story that I was eager to look like I was 'doing well' in the earlier stages of my working life. In buying things to appear to others like I was successful, I was spending money I didn't have. A lot of it was borrowed money from the banks, and I found myself in a position where I had a sizeable debt across credits cards and loans. Whilst I looked like I was doing okay, behind the scenes my finances were a mess. Every day you meet people that give the impression they're rich or well off through their material possessions but scratch the surface and often there's a big debt behind it all. Many people jump the gun and make premature and uneducated financial decisions without really knowing what they're getting themselves into.

What about you? What does your debt situation look like? If you don't have debts, then great, the message is to just steer clear. If you do have debts, then it's vital that you take the right actions to get rid of them.

Working your way to being debt free is not only an amazing feeling, but the new habits you develop along the way are perfect for when you are ready to begin building wealth.

In this chapter I am going to talk you through some useful approaches you can use to free yourself from debt as quickly as possible, as well as getting on the road to building a secure financial future!

From this point onwards, reject debt and the weight it places on your shoulders. Otherwise, it will eventually drive you into the ground. Get rid of all your credit cards and stop carrying them around with you.

The first thing to understand about debt is that there is good debt and there is bad debt. It is important to understand the key differences, so you are able to tell for yourself in the future what debt to avoid.

Good debt:

Used to buy things that increase in value & have low interest rates. A good example of this would be a mortgage for a property.

Bad debt:

Used to buy things that have very little value, or that go down in value. Usually have higher interest rates. Some examples of bad debt are credit cards, personal loans, overdrafts, pay day loans.

Why paying off bad debts is the priority

Having debt is bad for your mental wellbeing.

The idea of being below zero can be very disheartening and you can easily end up in a rut.

As you start to pay off your debt, it will have huge psychological benefits.

Owing nothing to anyone is an amazing feeling.

Strategies to pay down debt effectively

Strategy 1:

If you have good enough credit rating that you can get a 0% credit card.

1. Consolidation:

   a. Consolidate your debts onto a 0% credit card.

2. How to pay it down:

As previously discussed, a sensible amount to pay yourself first would be 10% of your income (this percentage can be whatever you decide it's just whatever works best for you). Whatever that amount is, it should eliminate your debt. There are two methods to do this depending on your preference and what will give the biggest feeling of progression:

   a) Use the whole 10% towards paying down the debt – this will pay down the debt quicker.

   b) Use half of the 10% to pay down the debt and half of the 10% to start building your investments – this way you are making progress on your future whilst getting yourself out of debt. However, it will take more time for the debt to be cleared.

I think a good way to think about method 'a' and 'b' above is that if you have relatively low debts and you think you can get them paid off within a year, then use method 'a'. If your debts are high and it's looking like it will take you years to pay off the debt, then use method 'b', because if it's going to be years before you can even start to save and invest, then you might get discouraged and just give up. Once you've set the amount to pay off put it to the side, and resume working on saving and investing for the future too – it will have a much more positive feeling.

It should be noted that 0% credit cards generally have a promotional term on them, meaning the 0% will only last for a certain period of time. Therefore, you should be aware when the promotional offer will end, so you are able to switch the balance to another 0% card before the end of the term if you were unable to clear the debt in time.

It is important you take note of this because the interest charged after the 0% promotional period ends can be high.

If you can't get the 0%, this strategy can also be applied if you are able to consolidate your debts onto a lower interest rate card or loan than you're currently paying to get the interest down as much as you can. If you do use this strategy, make sure you cut up and get rid of all your old cards so you dont use them again - it's very important that you do this!

There will also be a fee for moving / consolidating your debts so make sure you check what this is and factor it in.

Strategy 2:

If you do not have a good enough credit rating and cannot get a 0% or lower interest credit card.

In some cases, people might not have good enough credit rating and will not be approved for a 0% card to consolidate the debts. In this situation the debt repayment strategy will differ slightly.

1. Reduce the interest:

  a) Contact your lenders and see if they can offer you a better rate (lower rate) on the interest. Sometimes if you mention that another company is offering you a better rate, they might try to match it or beat it.

  It's a long-shot, but worth a try.

2. Minimum payments:

  a) Set all debts to minimum payments.

3. Additional Payments:

  a) Then work out how much extra you can put aside to pay off debts. Remember the concept of paying yourself first, and the appropriate percentage this should be relative to your income. The amount decided should always be used for paying down debt, and the following methods are both viable options in doing this, depending on your preferences.

  b) Use the whole 10% towards paying down the debt – this will pay down the debt quicker; or

  c) Use half of the 10% to pay down the debt and half of the 10% to start building your investments – this way you are making progress on your future whilst getting yourself out of debt. However, it will take more time for the debt to be cleared.

4. Smallest Debt first:

   a) Start paying the amount you have decided towards the smallest debt first, on top of the minimum payment.

5. Next Smallest Debt:

   a. Once the smallest debt is cleared, you are then able to use all the money you were originally using to pay off the smallest debt (including the minimum payment) and apply it to the next smallest debt. And you continue this process until each debt is cleared!

This particular strategy is best explained as 'The Debt Snowball' by Dave Ramsey.

You can see more in-depth details of this strategy of paying down debt here: https://www.ramseysolutions.com/debt/get-out-of-debt-with-the-debt-snowball-plan

In my experience this one of the most effective ways to clear your debts.

Common questions

1. In strategy 2 why would I not start paying down the debts with highest interest first?

This is down to the positive psychological impact and accomplishment you will get from clearing a debt, and the encouragement it will inspire to continue. One of the greatest motivators for people is progress. Through paying down the smallest debt first, you will get the feeling of progression sooner and you are more likely to carry on.

2. How can I pay down my debts quicker?

Reducing expenses elsewhere and redirecting the money towards paying down debt.

Perhaps sell some things that you no longer have use for to raise funds.

Finding a way to generate another income, whether you learn a new skill to increase your earning ability, or get a second job for a short period

The faster you eradicate the bad debt, the better, hence why I would apply all additional money that becomes available to clear these debts as quickly as possible. Whilst it is often difficult to pay off debts due to the change in habits and lifestyle it requires, the benefits outweigh the hardships tenfold.

I cannot express enough, how much it will be worth the effort!

BUILDING BLOCK 4 –
FINANCIAL PROTECTION

The idea of financial protection describes the insurances that can be put in place to protect you and your family financially.

Financial protection is continuously overlooked by many people, and it's difficult to express the importance of financial protection in the event of a life disaster, until it is too late. The issue with insurance is that it feels like you are paying for something that you hope to never make use of. However, if you are in a position where you need insurance, you will be extremely thankful for it. One of the most common things that people want when it comes to finances is a feeling of security – yet most of them don't have insurance. Therefore, financial protection is a crucial element to aid your "Flow State", due to how it encourages the peace of mind within.

There are different insurances that suit different people and their varying circumstances, such as relationship status, and whether they're a homeowner. I will explain the three main types of financial protection to be explored, to help establish what is right path for you. With that being said, for a bespoke solution and advice tailored to you, a meeting with your own adviser will help you put these ideas into practice. You can meet with an adviser like myself or find a protection specialist. It is not only cost effective, but an efficient way to spend your time. Often people may require a combination of different insurances, and this is a plan an adviser would be able to construct for you with ease.

Three main things to insure against & the type of insurance:

    1. Death – Life Insurance

    2. Accident or illness – Income Protection

    3. Serious/Critical Illness – Critical illness cover

As mentioned earlier, the insurances that apply to you will depend on what stage of life you're at, and your personal circumstances.

Life Insurance

There are a few key things to understand about life insurance.

Term

Term Life Insurance is when you take out life insurance for a specific amount of time. For example, you might want to take out life insurance for the same term as your mortgage, to ensure that your loved ones have enough money to pay off the mortgage in the event of your death. The term really amounts to your circumstances and what the life insurance is actually for.

There are 2 types of term:

1. Lump Sum
2. Family Income Benefit

Lump Sum – (Can be Fixed or Decreasing)

Fixed – You choose the lump sum figure that would like for your insurance cover, and this is the amount that is paid out regardless of when you die, within the term that you have set.

Decreasing – The lump sum figure you choose at the start of your insurance plan decreases over the term you have set. People often use these with their repayment mortgages, to the level of insurance decreasing in line with how much they owe back on the mortgage. Generally, premiums are lower with a decreasing term.

Family Income Benefit

Family Income Benefit is a type of life insurance that gives an income to your family for the remainder of term, instead of the lump sum pay out. For instance, you could take out a policy with a twenty-five-year term, paying £2000 to your family a month to support them in the event of your death. If you died five years after taking out the policy, it would pay out £2,000 per month for twenty years. However, if you died twenty years after taking out the policy, it would pay out £2,000 per month for five years instead.

Whole of life

Whole of Life insurance pays out regardless of when you die. This type of insurance is normally used for something specific like covering an inheritance tax bill.

Income Protection

Income protection is extremely valuable and very important in most cases. Out of everything, you are most likely to be unable to work due to accident or illness, making this a no brainer, it would be foolish to not have it. Having this type of protection allows you to remain financially stable, should you not be able to work in the event of a serious illness or injury. You can still pay your mortgage, pay your bills and support yourself through income protection.

The key things to know are:

It pays out on accident & illness.

It pays roughly 50% - 70% of your Gross income (income before tax).

It usually pays monthly (like a salary).

Premiums will depend on how risky you are – for example a roofer will be at higher risk of an accident than an office worker.

Premiums will also be based on several different factors like the ones mentioned above.

If you are employed and get sick pay, you can set a deferred period so that the insurance pay-out will not start until your sick pay stops – this helps bring the premium down.

Most people usually cover themselves until retirement age – this is highly dependent on an individual's personal circumstances and affordability.

Critical Illness Cover

The key thing to remember with critical illness cover, is that it covers specified serious illnesses. This type of cover pays out a lump sum on diagnosis of serious illnesses such as, a heart attack, stroke, or cancer. The terms of the policy will specify which illnesses you will covered for in that particular policy.

People often take out this type of insurance with this idea of covering their mortgage (which is most people's biggest liability), in the event of them becoming too ill to work. It can also be used to cover the costs of adaptations that might need to be made on the home because of the illness. Understanding what you need can get a bit tricky, so once again speak to a specialist to work out what's right for you specifically.

Just to explain

The explanation given on the different kinds of financial protection is a high level, potentially overwhelming overview. However, the main purpose behind this chapter, is to highlight the importance of having the correct protection (insurance) in place to protect yourself, and your family.

Flow State Money is all about being able to live life with as little worry as possible from a financial perspective, and that can only have its full effect if you have everything covered. Through being covered you can be in control and ready for any unlikely event, bringing the peace of mind desired. This makes financial protection (insurance) a vitally important part of developing a solid financial grounding for the future.

Just to reiterate, the type of financial protection that will be right for you will depend on your personal circumstances. For some people that might just need one type of protection and for others it might make sense for them to have a blend of the different types of protection. That's why I say it's probably wise to just speak with a Financial Planner or Protection Specialist that will be able to put together a bespoke packaged solution that will meet all your needs, at a premium that you're happy to pay and it doesn't usually cost any extra.

BUILDING BLOCK 5 – DESIGNING THE LIFE YOU WANT

Although this is building block five from a financial and investment planning perspective, this is probably one of the first things you should do personally. It will make things clearer, by mapping out what you are doing, so you know that you are on the right track.

Mastering the skill of goal setting will have a positive impact on your life overall. It will have a powerful effect over you and pull you in the direction of your best intentions.

We are affected in many ways by different things in life, from life events to the knowledge we obtain, we are constantly being nurtured by our environment. However, there is one element that despite its importance, is often overlooked, and that is our view of the future. In order you to make the right decisions daily that keep you in the right direction, your future must be considered. Setting a goal and working back from that goal helps you understand the actions you need to take now.

Money is a tool that helps you achieve the things that you want to achieve in life, but without knowing what they are, it just becomes aimless, and you will never feel like you are getting anywhere – because you don't know where you are going. You wouldn't just jump in your car and start driving without a destination. You will end up somewhere, but my bet is that it won't be where you want to be. This does not bring the feeling of being in a 'Flow State' or being in control. Therefore, goal setting is a vital element that should be implemented into your life if you want to achieve your version of financial success.

<u>There are 2 ways to face the future:</u>

1. With uncertainty (fear, worry, doubt, confusion)
2. With certainty (exciting, intentional, liberating, hope)

I know which one I would rather.

Without goals set, it's likely that you'll buy into someone else's views or ideas and end up living a life that's not really your own. The bottom line is, having a well thought out future will have a massive influence on you.

Picture your goals as a magnet, pulling you in the direction of the life you aspire to. The more defined, specific, and calculated your goals are, the more direct the path to the success you've envisioned will become.

Setting goals is one thing but in order for them to mean anything or have any power over you, you need to be clear on the reasons these goals are personally important. Their individual importance will become the driving force behind any action taken in working towards your goals. There are many reasons why a goal might be important to you, for example, the way it will make you feel, recognition, or maybe a better life for your family – often we are more driven to do things for other people than we are for ourselves.

More often than not, people are much smarter than what their bank balance may suggest. This can be due to the fact that their personal reasons haven't been discovered yet, and thus they don't have the drive to take any steps to improve their financial situation. So, decide what you want, write it down and be clear on your reasons – I'll talk you through a strategy that you can use to get this done, as a starting point.

Once you envisage what you want and where you'd like to go, you can then begin to use the income at your disposal to serve you and this vision. It is important to view the money as serving you, as opposed to chasing it and serving the money itself. People do this without a real purpose and are often left unfulfilled. However, by adjusting your perspective, and having your money serve you, through making intentional & meaningful decisions, you are able to regain control and freedom which is the whole idea behind 'Flow State Money'.

Once again, this part is vitally important for you to truly move forward in the right direction with your money management and start to make a real difference. By mastering this idea, whilst engaging with the strategies featured in this book, you will feel the compelling effects on your life.

Goal setting strategy

There are many ways that you can do this, but I will share a method I've employed and found to be particularly useful. This goal setting strategy is inspired by Jim Rohn.

This is very simple – decide what you want within the next 10 years and write it down!

Some things that might help inspire some ideas:

- Changes you'd like to make...
- How much you'd like to earn...
- How much you like to save...
- Habits you'd like to drop...
- Habits you'd like to acquire...
- Skills you want to teach your children...
- People you want to meet...
- The places you want to go...
- The places you want to see...
- What you want to be...
- What you want to share...
- What you want to have...
- Properties...
- Investments...
- Contribution to society...
- Projects you'd like to support...
- What you want to be known for...
- What you want to learn...

With this exercise imagine money is no object. It's important you write down all the things you want and not all things you believe you can afford. Explore your mind and collect your thoughts. Anywhere between thirty and fifty ideas written down would be good to work with.

1. Decide how long you think each goal will take and then write the number down next to it (just 1, 3, 5, 10 for the number of years), if it's less than a year just put 1.

2. Count how many 1's, 3's, 5's and 10's there are and write that down.

3. On your list of 1-year goals – pick out the 5 most important and write them in a list separately.

4. Write down why these goals are important to you! Remember earlier I mentioned about the reasons being the driving force. When the 'why' is strong, the taking action part is much easier!

5. Ask yourself this question: What person do I need to become, in order to achieve what I want?

Whatever way you decide to set your goals, it is important to record them and review the list frequently.
This exercise is a useful way to find direction, by collating and quantifying your goals. Though it may take an hour, it is time well spent, and put towards securing the future
you're aspiring to.

You can complete task this on the same worksheet you that you will have received from the Flow State Money Mindset chapter.

The beginning phases

Once you have completed the above task, it's likely you'll be feeling energised and hopefully feel a new sense of purpose and clarity on what you need to do. Most people at this stage are eager to get started.

However, there can often be a reality check too, and it might be that you've established you need to change direction, or perhaps learn a new skill to increase your earning ability. You will almost definitely be met with decisions that need to be made. Whatever those decisions happen to be, it would be beneficial to begin working on them straight away, otherwise you risk losing the newfound energy, or falling victim to doubts in the back of your mind if you leave it too long to take action.

With regards to the money management aspects, it is likely your goals will look like the ones featured below, in order to secure the financial grounding needed to then get started on your saving and investment journey for the future.

1. Get debt repayments up to date
2. Starter emergency fund (refer to chapter 2)
3. Pay down all debt (refer to chapter 3)
4. Save a fully funded emergency fund (refer to chapter 2)
5. Start saving and investing

BUILDING BLOCK 6 - SAVING AND INVESTING – GETTING STARTED

S aving and investing is where financial planning starts to get really exciting, because this is the part where you start to build upon your grounding.

Understanding how to invest and what types of investment are best for you is something a Financial Planner can assist with, similarly to financial protection.

However, this chapter will help you to understand about investing more, the power of investing over time, and the importance of investing in relation to your financial planning.

Differences

Firstly, I think it is important for you understand the basic difference between saving and investing.

Saving	Investing
◦ Short-medium term (1-5 years)	◦ Long term (5+years)
◦ Cash held in a bank or building society	◦ Assets (*I will explain more about these later*)
◦ Interest	◦ Investment returns
◦ Quickly accessible	◦ Usually for longer term
◦ Practically no risk, so no growth	◦ Involves risk & risk management in return for growth over the long term
◦ Usually, no cost	◦ Costs involved when investing
◦ Savings are influenced by the base rate – so basically you shop around for the best rate	◦ Investing is much more complicated and there's a lot more to it, so it requires a greater level of knowledge and understanding

Why invest?

Investing allows the value of your money to grow and puts your money to work to generate you returns. This money can be used for retirement, doing things for loved ones, and meeting financial objectives etc.

If your money is sitting in cash, there is a good chance that it is being eroded over time. With the current rates of inflation, and the low interest rates from the banks, your money is losing spending power the longer it sits in cash.

Put simply - inflation rates are the rates affecting the prices of goods, and interest rates are the level of return the bank gives you for holding your money.

So, if the rates of inflation (costs of goods) are going up by 3% per year, but your bank's interest rate is only 0.5% per year, then the value of your money is effectively decreasing by 2.5% per year. (3% - 0.5% = 2.5%)

Just to put that into perspective

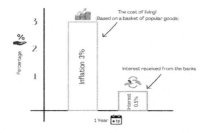

Diagram 4 (repeated)

Say you have £10,000 in the bank and assume interest
rates of 0.5%

Years	3% inflation
1	£9,750.000
3	£9,268.59
5	£8,810.96
10	£7,763.30
15	£6,840.21
20	£6,026.88
25	£5,310.26

Table 1

The table above reiterates the idea that by leaving your money in cash, it is just eroding over time, with low interest rates and higher inflation rates.

In ten years, your money is worth roughly ¾'s of what it is worth now. In twenty-five years, your money is worth basically half of what it is worth now – effectively, everything will cost twice as much.

This alone is enough of a reason to invest, so your money can get returns to at least keep up with inflation and maintain the spending power of your money.

These figures used are just as examples for the illustration and we will vary from year to year.

Understanding the different components

Assets

An asset is something we buy that can increase or decrease in value. The aim is to buy assets that increase in value over time, so we must think carefully about the assets we buy.

Main Asset Classes

1.Cash

Typically, this is money held in bank and building society accounts. Considered very low risk and therefore the rate of return on interest is low, though it can vary depending on the state of the economy. The rate of interest return is unlikely to keep up with the rate of inflation over the long-term.

2. Property

This can be residential property or commercial property. Many people will build personal property portfolios that can generate an income, as well the hope for capital growth over time. You can also invest in a diversified portfolio of commercial property through an investment fund. These types of investments are usually excellent for the purpose of income but can also be excellent for capital growth over a period of time. They are typically illiquid, meaning the property usually needs to be sold before you can realise any profit and access your money, which can take time. Property will tend to fluctuate (rise and fall) in value over time, but generally less than investment in stocks and shares.

3. Bonds

There are 2 main types of bonds to be aware of, government bonds and corporate bonds. The bonds are offered by a government or company in order to raise finance, whilst offering investors a set rate of return over a chosen period of time (term). The original capital amount invested is then returned at the end of the term.

There is risk involved, because the bonds are linked to the financial strength of the organisation (government or company). Consequently, the return is typically higher than the interest you would receive in cash. Bonds are still considered a lower risk investment, but a higher risk than cash.

Government issued bonds (Gilts) are seen as the lowest risk, as the likelihood of a government failing is less than a company, thus reducing the risk.

Company issued bonds (corporate bonds) can vary in the level of risk depending on the size and strength of the company issuing the bond.

4. Equities (Stocks and Shares)

Investing in stocks and shares means that you are buying a share of a company, therefore owning a portion of the company. The value of that share will depend on the overall performance and value of the company. History shows that investments in stocks and shares provided higher returns over the long term, but they fluctuate (rise and fall) the most. Some stocks and shares are higher risk than others based on factors such as where in the world the companies are, to the type of industry they are in. For example, it's likely that stocks and shares bought in lesser-developed economies will be higher risk than stocks and shares in the United States.

Though stocks and shares have been proven to provide the highest rate of return over time, they are considered higher risk, they are the most volatile and the returns are not guaranteed. Risk management is imperative when investing.

5. Alternatives & Commodities

Alternative investment and commodities tend to include things such as oil, gold, silver, timber, coffee etc...
These are typically considered higher risk and usually only make up a small part of an investor's portfolio.

Funds

Investment assets can be held in funds which are managed by a professional fund manager or fund management company. You can also get tracker funds that track the market.

When you invest in a fund, your money in invested alongside many other investors. Your funds are pooled together with the group, then allowing you to purchase a vast range of varying assets, stocks, and shares.

The upside to investing through a fund is the added ability to diversify, and a reduction in risk that comes as a result of being in a group.

<u>Accounts & Tax Wrappers</u>

Funds are held in investment accounts. You can have an unwrapped investment account or a tax wrapped investment account (tax wrappers).

When your investments grow and produce returns, you can be liable to be taxed on the growth or the income. If you hold your funds in an unwrapped investment account, then you are likely to be liable to tax at some stage in your investment journey – which can be a big drain on your investment returns.

If you have a HMRC approved tax wrapped investment account, then you can wipe out or significantly reduce any tax liabilities.

<u>The 2 main tax wrappers to pay attention to are:</u>

1. Pension
2. Investment ISA

The tax benefits of these two tax wrappers are very important to understand and they can potentially change each financial year, therefore the benefits won't be discussed due to the fact they could be different by the time you read this. The main thing is to understand is that they are very important in your investment journey and plenty of people have become millionaires utilising these two tax wrappers alone.

It would be beneficial to do some research at the time of reading this or speak with a professional financial planner to help you understand the benefits in greater detail.

Alternatively, you can email in to request a call back and either me or one of the team will happily talk you through the tax benefits of these tax wrappers at the time.

I am qualified to advise based on UK tax laws; therefore, I can only advise if you are based in the UK or have UK based tax wrappers. If you are from outside of the UK, then I would suggest speaking to a professional financial planner in your respective countries.

There are other tax wrappers that could be considered at later stages of financial planning, but I don't feel it's necessary for the purpose of this book.

Platforms

Platforms are an administration system that allow you to hold different types of accounts in one place.

Understanding risk

Investing is heavily influenced by risk management. There is a risk in everything we do, but that doesn't mean we should shy away. When investing, risk is not something to try and avoid – if you avoid risk, then you avoid any chance of growth and investment returns. Risk is something you should learn to both understand and manage, with the correct risk management, risk can be used massively in your favour.

Once again, liaising with a financial planner for this segment will be beneficial for your journey, as they will be able to help you understand what investments are right for you and how to diversify. This process can be time consuming if you decide to do it alone, that's not to say that it is impossible, it's just that having a financial planner will make it much easier for you, and a lot less time-consuming. The reason it is not time efficient is because there is plenty to understand before making your investment decision, including how to diversify and the level of risk you should take. On top of this, you then have to monitor and regularly review your investments. By using a Financial Planner, you can harness the knowledge and experience they have already garnered to help make your decisions.

There are many risks to consider, but the main risk to consider is the risk of loss. However, there is also reward for the risk and you are only truly at a loss if the investments are sold when the investment value is down. There are different levels of risk that you can take, no-risk, low, lower medium, medium, higher medium and high. Levels of risk are crucial to understand and manage, however, they should not be a reason to not invest.

In fact, not investing at all is a risk in itself, as you are guaranteeing yourself no chance of growth on your money. With the high rates of inflation vs low interest rates, the value of your money will simply be eaten away if it just sits in cash.

Ways to reduce risk

Diversification (Very important!)

Diversify your investments. The saying goes – "Don't place all of your eggs in one basket". There are many ways to diversify your investments, across asset classes, geographically, sectors, different fund managers to name a few. By spreading your money around, you are minimising your level of risk, through considering how some investments will perform better or worse than others at different times.

Time

Different timescales will mean different levels of risk. The longer you hold your investments; the higher level of risk can potentially be taken (depending on your investment objective). The reason for this is because there is plenty of time for the investment to grow and recover from any dips we might see in the market.

Investment returns over time

I am in the UK, so I am going to show you an example of what regular investments in the FTSE 100 (UK Index) looks like based on an average return.

The FTSE 100 (Financial Times Stock Exchange 100) is an index made up of the 100 biggest public companies that can be traded on the London Stock Exchange.

So, for example if you were to invest in the FTSE 100 you would be investing in the performance of the UK's top 100 companies – commonly referred to as blue chip companies.

FTSE 100 performance over 25-year periods

Looking at all the possible 25-year holding periods since the FTSE 100's start shows an average annualised (yearly) return of +8.33%.

The worst return over 25 years was +6.43% annualised

The highest return was +9.99% annualised, between 31 December 1985 and 31 December 2010.

As shown in the chart on the next page.

FTSE 100 performance over 25-year periods

	Total return	Total annualised
Worst	+375.31%	+6.43%
Best	+981.38%	+9.99%
Average	+657.81%	+8.33%
Median	+606.10%	+8.13%

Source: IG

Caution: I am using the FTSE 100 purely because it's easy to use as an example and most people have heard of it. Just to be clear this is an example to illustrate what small regular investments over time can look like and is not a promise of what will happen as the returns are not guaranteed. They could be higher, or they could be lower. Also, investing purely in one index may not suitable for each persons specific requirements and risk tolerance.

You may have heard of term *compounding?* There is a book written by an author called Darren Hardy, who explains 'the compound effect' brilliantly – it's a great book and I would encourage you to read it. The compound effect is the strategy of reaping huge rewards from small, seemingly insignificant actions.

In this example we will explore the rewards granted from making small 'seemingly insignificant' investments over time, to show you the power of compounding investment returns. Using the best (9.99% annualised return), the average (8.33% annualised return) and worst (6.43% annualised return) that we looked at above for the FTSE 100 over all the possible 25 year holding periods.

This is based on an annual (yearly) investment of £2,400, or another way to look at it £200 per month.

Best (9.99%)

	Investing at age 19 with 9.99% return (annualised)			Investing at age 30 with 9.99% return (annualised)		
	Age	Annual Investment	Total Value	Total Value	Annual Investment	Age	
Start →	19	£2,400	£2,640	£0	£0	19
	20	£2,400	£5,543	£0	£0	20
	21	£2,400	£8,737	£0	£0	21
	22	£2,400	£12,249	£0	£0	22
	23	£2,400	£16,113	£0	£0	23
	24	£2,400	£20,362	£0	£0	24
	25	£2,400	£25,036	£0	£0	25
	26	£2,400	£30,177	£0	£0	26
	27	£2,400	£35,831	£0	£0	27
Stop and leave to grow →	28	£2,400	£42,051	£0	£0	28
	29	£2,400	£48,891	£0	£0	29
	30	£0	£53,776	£2,640	£2,400	30	← Start
	31	£0	£59,148	£5,543	£2,400	31
	32	£0	£65,057	£8,737	£2,400	32
	33	£0	£71,556	£12,249	£2,400	33
	34	£0	£78,704	£16,113	£2,400	34
	35	£0	£86,567	£20,362	£2,400	35
	36	£0	£95,215	£25,036	£2,400	36
	37	£0	£104,727	£30,177	£2,400	37
	38	£0	£115,189	£35,831	£2,400	38
	39	£0	£126,697	£42,051	£2,400	39
	40	£0	£139,354	£48,891	£2,400	40
	41	£0	£153,275	£56,415	£2,400	41
	42	£0	£168,587	£64,691	£2,400	42
	43	£0	£185,429	£73,794	£2,400	43
	44	£0	£203,953	£83,805	£2,400	44
	45	£0	£224,328	£94,817	£2,400	45
	46	£0	£246,739	£106,929	£2,400	46
	47	£0	£271,388	£120,251	£2,400	47
	48	£0	£298,500	£134,904	£2,400	48
	49	£0	£328,320	£151,021	£2,400	49
	50	£0	£361,119	£168,747	£2,400	50
	51	£0	£397,195	£188,245	£2,400	51
	52	£0	£436,874	£209,690	£2,400	52
	53	£0	£480,518	£233,278	£2,400	53
	54	£0	£528,522	£259,223	£2,400	54
	55	£0	£581,321	£287,759	£2,400	55
	56	£0	£639,395	£319,145	£2,400	56
	57	£0	£703,271	£353,668	£2,400	57
	58	£0	£773,527	£391,639	£2,400	58
	59	£0	£850,803	£433,404	£2,400	59
	60	£0	£935,798	£479,340	£2,400	60
	61	£0	£1,029,284	£529,866	£2,400	61
	62	£0	£1,132,110	£585,440	£2,400	62
	63	£0	£1,245,208	£646,565	£2,400	63
	64	£0	£1,369,604	£713,796	£2,400	64
	65	£0	£1,506,427	VS £787,744	£2,400	65	← Stop
Total you invested →			£26,400	£86,400			← Total you invested

Earnings on your investment
£1,480,027

Earnings on your investment
£701,344

Investing at 19 you earn	£1,480,027
Investing at 30 you earn	£701,344
You earn this much more starting at 19 and stopping at 30	£778,683

Note: Also look at the 'Total you invested' for each and you will see that you invest £60,000 less starting from age 19 (that's a *quarter* of the amount than if you start at age 30!!)

Start investing now rather later!

	Investing at age 19 with 8.33% return (annualised)			Average (8.33%)	Investing at age 30 with 8.33% return (annualised)		
	Age	Annual Investment	Total Value		Total Value	Annual Investment	Age
Start →	19	£2,400	£2,600		£0	£0	19
	20	£2,400	£5,416		£0	£0	20
	21	£2,400	£8,468		£0	£0	21
	22	£2,400	£11,773		£0	£0	22
	23	£2,400	£15,353		£0	£0	23
	24	£2,400	£19,232		£0	£0	24
	25	£2,400	£23,434		£0	£0	25
	26	£2,400	£27,986		£0	£0	26
	27	£2,400	£32,917		£0	£0	27
Stop and leave to grow →	28	£2,400	£38,259		£0	£0	28
	29	£2,400	£44,046		£0	£0	29
	30	£0	£47,715		£2,600	£2,400	30 ← Start
	31	£0	£51,690		£5,416	£2,400	31
	32	£0	£55,996		£8,468	£2,400	32
	33	£0	£60,660		£11,773	£2,400	33
	34	£0	£65,713		£15,353	£2,400	34
	35	£0	£71,187		£19,232	£2,400	35
	36	£0	£77,117		£23,434	£2,400	36
	37	£0	£83,541		£27,986	£2,400	37
	38	£0	£90,500		£32,917	£2,400	38
	39	£0	£98,038		£38,259	£2,400	39
	40	£0	£106,205		£44,046	£2,400	40
	41	£0	£115,052		£50,315	£2,400	41
	42	£0	£124,636		£57,106	£2,400	42
	43	£0	£135,018		£64,463	£2,400	43
	44	£0	£146,265		£72,433	£2,400	44
	45	£0	£158,449		£81,067	£2,400	45
	46	£0	£171,647		£90,419	£2,400	46
	47	£0	£185,946		£100,551	£2,400	47
	48	£0	£201,435		£111,527	£2,400	48
	49	£0	£218,214		£123,417	£2,400	49
	50	£0	£236,392		£136,298	£2,400	50
	51	£0	£256,083		£150,251	£2,400	51
	52	£0	£277,415		£165,367	£2,400	52
	53	£0	£300,523		£181,742	£2,400	53
	54	£0	£325,557		£199,481	£2,400	54
	55	£0	£352,676		£218,698	£2,400	55
	56	£0	£382,054		£239,515	£2,400	56
	57	£0	£413,879		£262,067	£2,400	57
	58	£0	£448,355		£286,497	£2,400	58
	59	£0	£485,703		£312,962	£2,400	59
	60	£0	£526,162		£341,631	£2,400	60
	61	£0	£569,991		£372,689	£2,400	61
	62	£0	£617,472		£406,334	£2,400	62
	63	£0	£668,907		£442,782	£2,400	63
	64	£0	£724,627		£482,265	£2,400	64
	65	£0	£784,989	VS	£525,038	£2,400	65 ← Stop
Total you invested →			£26,400		£525,038	£86,400 ←	Total you invested

Earnings on your investment
£758,589

Earnings on your investment
£438,638

Investing at 19 you earn	→ £758,589
Investing at 30 you earn	→ £438,638
You earn this much more starting at 19 and stopping at 30	→ £319,950

Note: Also look at the 'Total you invested' for each and you will see that you invest £60,000 less starting from age 19 (that's a _quarter_ of the amount than if you start at age 30!!)

Start investing now rather later!

Worst (6.43%)

	Investing at age 19 with 6.43% return (annualised)				Investing at age 30 with 6.43% return (annualised)		
	Age	Annual Investment	Total Value		Total Value	Annual Investment	Age
Start →	19	£2,400	£2,554		£0	£0	19
	20	£2,400	£5,273		£0	£0	20
	21	£2,400	£8,166		£0	£0	21
	22	£2,400	£11,246		£0	£0	22
	23	£2,400	£14,523		£0	£0	23
	24	£2,400	£18,011		£0	£0	24
	25	£2,400	£21,724		£0	£0	25
	26	£2,400	£25,675		£0	£0	26
	27	£2,400	£29,880		£0	£0	27
Stop and leave to grow →	28	£2,400	£34,356		£0	£0	28
→	29	£2,400	£39,119		£0	£0	29
	30	£0	£41,634		£2,554	£2,400	30 ← Start
	31	£0	£44,311		£5,273	£2,400	31
	32	£0	£47,161		£8,166	£2,400	32
	33	£0	£50,193		£11,246	£2,400	33
	34	£0	£53,421		£14,523	£2,400	34
	35	£0	£56,855		£18,011	£2,400	35
	36	£0	£60,511		£21,724	£2,400	36
	37	£0	£64,402		£25,675	£2,400	37
	38	£0	£68,543		£29,880	£2,400	38
	39	£0	£72,951		£34,356	£2,400	39
	40	£0	£77,641		£39,119	£2,400	40
	41	£0	£82,634		£44,189	£2,400	41
	42	£0	£87,947		£49,584	£2,400	42
	43	£0	£93,602		£55,327	£2,400	43
	44	£0	£99,621		£61,439	£2,400	44
	45	£0	£106,026		£67,944	£2,400	45
	46	£0	£112,844		£74,867	£2,400	46
	47	£0	£120,099		£82,235	£2,400	47
	48	£0	£127,822		£90,077	£2,400	48
	49	£0	£136,041		£98,423	£2,400	49
	50	£0	£144,788		£107,306	£2,400	50
	51	£0	£154,098		£116,760	£2,400	51
	52	£0	£164,007		£126,822	£2,400	52
	53	£0	£174,552		£137,531	£2,400	53
	54	£0	£185,776		£148,929	£2,400	54
	55	£0	£197,721		£161,059	£2,400	55
	56	£0	£210,435		£173,970	£2,400	56
	57	£0	£223,966		£187,710	£2,400	57
	58	£0	£238,367		£202,334	£2,400	58
	59	£0	£253,694		£217,899	£2,400	59
	60	£0	£270,006		£234,464	£2,400	60
	61	£0	£287,368		£252,094	£2,400	61
	62	£0	£305,846		£270,858	£2,400	62
	63	£0	£325,511		£290,829	£2,400	63
	64	£0	£346,442		£312,084	£2,400	64
	65	£0	£368,718	VS	£334,705	£2,400	65 ← Stop
Total you invested →			£26,400		£86,400 ←		Total you invested

Earnings on your investment £342,318

Earnings on your investment £248,305

Investing at 19 you earn	→ £342,318
Investing at 30 you earn	→ £248,305
You earn this much more starting at 19 and stopping at 30	→ £94,013

Note: Also look at the 'Total you invested' for each and you will see that you invest £60,000 less starting from age 19 (that's a quarter of the amount than if you start at age 30!!)

Start investing now rather later!

In the charts, it is clear to see that if you started saving £200 per month at the age of 19 and stopped at age 29 (10 years), and then never contributed ever again, at 65 you'd still end up with more money in the pot than if you started at age 30 and contributed £200 per month until age 65 (35 years). Not only do you end up with more money in the pot, but significantly more.

The table clearly presents the benefit for investment, even if its smaller amounts to start with, the earlier you start the better. This doesn't mean that if you're thirty or forty years old and haven't started yet that you shouldn't try, it just requires a different approach and increasing those investment contributions. The next chart will be able to make things clearer on the topic.

The next chart helps to show you the power of compound investment returns.

Einstein said, "Compound interest is the 8th wonder of the world, he who understands it, earns it, he who doesn't, pays it."

If you are investing even a small portion of your money each time you get paid, allowing it to grow over time, you're becoming 'wealthier' even while you're sleeping – your money is now working for you.

COMPOUND INTEREST - 8TH WONDER OF THE WORLD						
Assumes Annualised Returns of 8%						
Contributions		Years				
Daily	Monthly	10	20	30	40	50
£5	£150	£28,162	£88,961	£220,223	£503,606	£1,115,409
£10	£300	£56,324	£177,923	£440,445	£1,007,212	£2,230,818
£20	£600	£112,648	£355,845	£880,890	£2,014,423	£4,461,637
£30	£900	£168,971	£533,768	£1,321,335	£3,021,635	£6,692,455
£40	£1,200	£225,295	£711,690	£1,761,780	£4,028,847	£8,923,273
£50	£1,500	£281,619	£889,613	£2,202,226	£5,036,059	£11,154,092

WHAT WILL IT TAKE TO BECOME A MILLIONAIRE BY AGE 65?		
Assumes Annualised Returns of 8%		
Age	Daily Saving	Monthly Saving	Yearly Saving
20	£6.25	£187.50	£2,250.00
25	£9.17	£275.00	£3,300.00
30	£13.75	£412.50	£4,950.00
35	£20.97	£629.17	£7,550.00
40	£32.22	£966.67	£11,600.00
45	£51.11	£1,533.33	£18,400.00
50	£84.86	£2,545.83	£30,550.00
55	£154.72	£4,641.67	£55,700.00

This chart is to give an indication of how much money you would need to be investing on a daily, monthly, or yearly basis to reach £1,000,000 by age 65 with a NET return of 8% Annualised Return.

1 Less Takeaway Night Per Month!?						
Assumes Annualised Returns of 8%						
One Takeaway cost	Over that year	10 Years	20 Years	30 Years	40 Years	50 Years
£30	£360.00	£5,632.38	£17,792.25	£44,044.51	£100,721.17	£223,081.84

All charts are purely to illustrate the power of compounded returns over time
and it is important to note that investment returns can vary and are not guaranteed
The rate of 8% has been used purely based on the average of the 25 year holding periods of the FTSE 100
discussed earlier in the chapter and is only used as an example

Freedom fund

As you can see in the last section, the compounding effect of investment returns can lead to some amazing figures. Of course, the more you invest the more of that compounding effect you are going to see and the bigger your pot is likely to be.

You'll remember that I previously discussed what I like to call the "freedom fund". This is actually a pension fund. I find that the word pension is quite off putting, as people associate them with old age and believing them to be complicated. With this in mind, it is important to understand the true value of the pension and the benefits of using it.

The vast majority of people work hard now to live the lifestyle they want to live, and one day not have to work, but still maintain that level of lifestyle. Some people say to me that they can't wait until the day they can stop working, whereas others endeavour to continue working as long as they can. Both are understandable aspirations, though most people in the later stages of life would rather be working out of choice than obligation because they cannot afford to stop. The whole point of saving and investing is to give you that freedom of choice. The truth is, what we want right now, in comparison to the future may differ, but if you are in a position where you have the 'freedom of choice', then you can do whatever you desire.

To be financially independent and live off the proceeds of your own resources is to be in the position where nothing or no one has a claim over your time. You are free to live as you wish. Whether that means working on a passion project, travelling, or spending more time with family, you have the means to do so. The point is that you are free to choose with no financial restrictions holding you back.

The pension is currently the most tax efficient way to build wealth in the UK. One of the biggest drains on government funds is support and care for elderly people, and it is only increasing as we are living longer as a species. Therefore, as an incentive - The Government give you tax relief on your pension contributions to encourage you save/invest for your future. This means people can support themselves financially in their retirement years as opposed to relying on The Government.

The tax relief for a basic rate taxpayer at this point is 20%. Referring back to the earlier example of £200's worth of contributions per month, if you were putting that into your pension pot, then the actual contribution amount would be £250 per month because HMRC will Gross it up by 20% (they give you the 20% tax back that you already paid on the money you earned).

Even though you've only invested £200 physically, the actual investment amount will be £250. That extra £50 each month compounded over time will make a massive difference to your pot.

Example

Your Contribution (you pay)	£200
20% Tax- relief (HMRC top-up)	£50
Total pension contribution	**£250**

To see the difference that the to-up from HMRC can make, see the next chart.

Not only do you get an uplift on your investment amount from the tax-relief, but your investments in the pension also grow income-tax-free and capital-gains-tax free.

When you invest in anything that produces an income, you're likely to be liable to income tax. For example, if you're invested in a fund that produces an income, income tax will have to be paid on that income, reducing the value, with less funds to benefit from the compound effect. Similarly, if you are invested in a growth fund, you will usually have to pay capital gains tax on the growth. However, when your investments are wrapped in the pension tax wrapper, they are shielded from those taxes. This protection means you have more money in the pot to benefit from that powerful compounding effect, which over the longer term will make a significant difference to the size of your pot.

When you eventually come to access your pension, there might be taxes to pay on exit, but that will be in relation to your tax status at the time and should be discussed with a financial planner/pension adviser when the time is necessary.

Average (8.33%)

	Investing at age 19 with 8.33% return (annualised)		Investing at age 30 with 8.33% return (annualised)		
Age	Annual Investment	Total Value	Total Value	Annual Investment	Age
19	£3,000	£3,250	£0	£0	19
20	£3,000	£6,771	£0	£0	20
21	£3,000	£10,584	£0	£0	21
22	£3,000	£14,716	£0	£0	22
23	£3,000	£19,192	£0	£0	23
24	£3,000	£24,040	£0	£0	24
25	£3,000	£29,293	£0	£0	25
26	£3,000	£34,983	£0	£0	26
27	£3,000	£41,147	£0	£0	27
28	£3,000	£47,824	£0	£0	28
29	£3,000	£55,058	£0	£0	29
30	£0	£59,644	£3,250	£3,000	30
31	£0	£64,612	£6,771	£3,000	31
32	£0	£69,995	£10,584	£3,000	32
33	£0	£75,825	£14,716	£3,000	33
34	£0	£82,141	£19,192	£3,000	34
35	£0	£88,984	£24,040	£3,000	35
36	£0	£96,396	£29,293	£3,000	36
37	£0	£104,426	£34,983	£3,000	37
38	£0	£113,125	£41,147	£3,000	38
39	£0	£122,548	£47,824	£3,000	39
40	£0	£132,756	£55,058	£3,000	40
41	£0	£143,815	£62,894	£3,000	41
42	£0	£155,795	£71,383	£3,000	42
43	£0	£168,772	£80,579	£3,000	43
44	£0	£182,831	£90,541	£3,000	44
45	£0	£198,061	£101,333	£3,000	45
46	£0	£214,559	£113,024	£3,000	46
47	£0	£232,432	£125,689	£3,000	47
48	£0	£251,794	£139,409	£3,000	48
49	£0	£272,768	£154,271	£3,000	49
50	£0	£295,490	£170,372	£3,000	50
51	£0	£320,104	£187,814	£3,000	51
52	£0	£346,769	£206,709	£3,000	52
53	£0	£375,654	£227,177	£3,000	53
54	£0	£406,946	£249,351	£3,000	54
55	£0	£440,845	£273,372	£3,000	55
56	£0	£477,567	£299,394	£3,000	56
57	£0	£517,349	£327,583	£3,000	57
58	£0	£560,444	£358,121	£3,000	58
59	£0	£607,129	£391,202	£3,000	59
60	£0	£657,703	£427,039	£3,000	60
61	£0	£712,489	£465,862	£3,000	61
62	£0	£771,840	£507,918	£3,000	62
63	£0	£836,134	£553,477	£3,000	63
64	£0	£905,784	£602,832	£3,000	64
65	£0	£981,236	£656,298	£3,000	65

Start → (age 19)
Stop and leave to grow → (age 29)
Start ← (age 30)
Stop ← (age 65)

VS (between £981,236 and £656,298)

Total you invested → £33,000

Total you invested ← £108,000

Earnings on your investment
£948,236

Earnings on your investment
£548,298

Investing at 19 you earn	£948,236
Investing at 30 you earn	£548,298
You earn this much more starting at 19 and stopping at 30	£399,938

Note: Also look at the 'Total you invested' for each and you will see that you invest £75,000 less starting from age 19 (that's a _quarter_ of the amount than if you start at age 30!!)

Start investing now rather later!

Looking at the difference in the example of the investment table earlier in the chapter (based on the <u>average</u> growth we saw of

8.33%), and the last investment table we just looked at (based on the same growth but just using the pension), it is clear that by using the pension tax wrapper there is an additional £196,247 (going by the investing at 19 side). On the 'investing at 30 side' the difference is £131,260.

That's just from the tax-relief that you are getting on your contributions, meaning this is from money that was not originally yours. Of course, the more you invest, the bigger that number will be.

These benefits are also available for higher rate and additional rate taxpayers too.

It's important to acknowledge that the rules surrounding tax-relief could change and might even vary slightly from the point that I wrote this. There are also contribution allowances and caps on those allowances which can vary on several different variables. The reliefs and allowances might differ for people depending on their personal tax status and wider circumstances – things tend to get trickier the more money you earn. The details of what affects tax relief are very in depth and don't concern the main goal of the book. I am purely trying to illustrate a point here to help inspire you to take action to make smart decisions for your financial future. I would strongly recommend speaking to a professional Financial Planner, whether you decide to reach out to us or someone else, it doesn't matter but it would be sensible for you to speak with a professional to find out what makes most sense for you before embarking on this part of your journey.

Once you have established how much you need to be investing each month to reach your objective or be able to stop working (have freedom of choice) then start the payments and forget about it – set it and forget it. What I mean by this, is set it up as a direct debit so that it goes out with your monthly outgoings and that way you don't have to think about it.

CLOSING SUMMARY

To summarise, the first thing to do is take the steps to get your financial grounding built and secure.

Then, work out how much is enough for you to have the freedom of choice at your chosen point in the future. From this you will be able to discover how much you should sensibly be investing each month. Once again, a good Financial Planner will be able to assist you with this.

You need to invest each month and set this as a direct debit payment to be included in your outgoings. Frequently review your plans and be secure in the fact you're taking all the steps necessary to secure your finances. Let your investments work for you in the background and keep feeding them gradually.

The bottom line is we all work so hard now so that one day we don't have to, and if we do work, at that point it will be out of choice rather than necessity. So, whatever you decide to do with your money once you have taken care of these responsible actions discussed above, is entirely up to you. Of course, many of you will have other objectives, whether that's saving for something (children, a car, a house, a holiday etc), investing further, or spending your money guilt free - knowing that you have taken care of all your main responsibilities each month. Get that Flow State feeling between yourself and your money.

As we come to a close on this book, I am aware that there is quite a lot of information to take on board and a lot to factor in. However, if you start to implement these building blocks gradually, you will notice a considerable difference.

Going through each of these building blocks will put you in a position where you have a solid financial grounding, and you will be ready to start your investment journey confidently. Building block 6 is just the beginning of understanding what could be possible for you and your finances.

If you have already started your investment journey, then use building blocks 1- 5 to underpin and review what you are already doing.

There are a vast number of benefits in getting on top of this area of your life, the proof will be in your progress, the peace of mind feeling you achieve and the rewards you reap through taking these steps.

As explained throughout the book, the purpose is to help inspire you get started in making smart decisions with your money that will have a life changing impact in the future. Paired with that is the certainty of knowing that you are taking the correct steps. Once your personal finances are of a certain size, things can get more complicated and that is when seeking professional financial advice is a must.

Lastly, I would like to congratulate you and thank you for taking the time to read this book. If you have managed to get this far you should feel proud, because you have already set yourself apart from most through beginning a journey most never properly start or start doing it properly way too late...

Good luck with your Flow State Money journey.

FINAL WORDS

Just a few final words from me. These are some realisations I had and some inspirational thoughts that helped me to get started and helped me along the way.

Get clear on what you want in life and then go and get it.

Don't wait for somebody to come and save you because no one's coming. Only you can do that.

Everyone is running their own race. Your starting point might be way further back than some other people's starting point so don't compare yourself and don't get disheartened. On the flipside don't judge someone else's progress because you don't know what their starting point was or the battles they've had to face.

> "REFUSE TO BELIEVE THAT THERE ANY CIRCUMSTANCES
> SUFFICIENTLY STRONG ENOUGH TO DEFEAT YOU IN THE
> ACCOMPLISHMENT OF YOUR PURPOSE"
>
> -   EARL NIGHTINGALE

ACKNOWLEDGEMENTS

I took inspiration from various sources. In particular, I would like to acknowledge Pete Matthew and thank him for his inspiration and his blessing to mention him in this book. I was hugely inspired by Pete and his podcast, the meaningful money podcast. I would highly recommend!

I would like thank:

All of you that had a positive contribution to my life and believed in me growing up. You'll know who you are!

Everyone that took the time to read my drafts and provided me with the genuine feedback I needed.

A special mention to:

My partner Sophie and my son Romy for always rooting for me. Lots of love to you both x